The Double-Symmetrical Augmented Scale for Jazz Improvisation

by Xabier Oró

Online Audio

To access the online audio recording go to:

WWW.MELBAY.COM/30968MEB

WWW.MELBAY.COM

Credits:

Music recording, mixing and mastering by Carles Delgado
Text editing by Marc Aliana
Photography by Aladid Studios
Artwork and cover design by Enric Punsola: www.enricpunsola.com

With the support of:

esmuc
ESCOLA SUPERIOR DE MÚSICA DE CATALUNYA

www.esmuc.cat

About the Author

Xabier "Xabi" Oró is a musician and music educator from Barcelona, Spain. After studying at l'AULA de Música Moderna i Jazz del Conservatori del Liceu, he was granted a scholarship to attend Berklee College of Music in Boston, where he graduated summa cum laude in Guitar Performance. Upon returning to Barcelona, he earned a Master's Degree in Jazz Guitar Performance from the Catalonia College of Music (ESMUC).

Through the years, Xabi has been mentored by internationally acclaimed musicians such as: Tim Miller, Mick Goodrick, David Fiucynsky, David Gilmore, Ed Tomassi, Dave Santoro, Bret Wilmott, Dani Pérez, and Rick Dimuzio. He has also collaborated with artists across a wide range of genres, showcasing his unique blend of rock, jazz, and fusion.

Xabi Oro's website:
http://www.xabioro.com

Acknowledgements

I am obliged to like to thank my friends, familly and colleagues for their support and inspiration.

Special thanks to:

Paco Salas and Pep Mateu, for teaching me the basics of music.
Dani Pérez, for his invaluable help with this book.
Isaac Romagosa, for motivation.
Xavier Oró, for his many beneficial suggestions.
Yaiza Gutiérrez, for her unwavering support.
Mikel Oró, for believing in me.
Pau Oró, for linguistic advice.
Allan Holdsworth, for his priceless inspiration.

Table of Contents

Audio Contents

TRACKS

Recommended Background

Having a practical understanding of harmony, chord-scales (modes), chord progressions, and sight-reading will help you maximize the benefits of studying the material in this book. Likewise, I recommend being familiar with the music vocabulary of early improvisational styles, such as blues, rhythm, swing, bebop, etc.

Chord Symbol Notation

Chord symbol notation it is not completely standardized: Below are the notation used in this book and some alternate options that you may encounter:

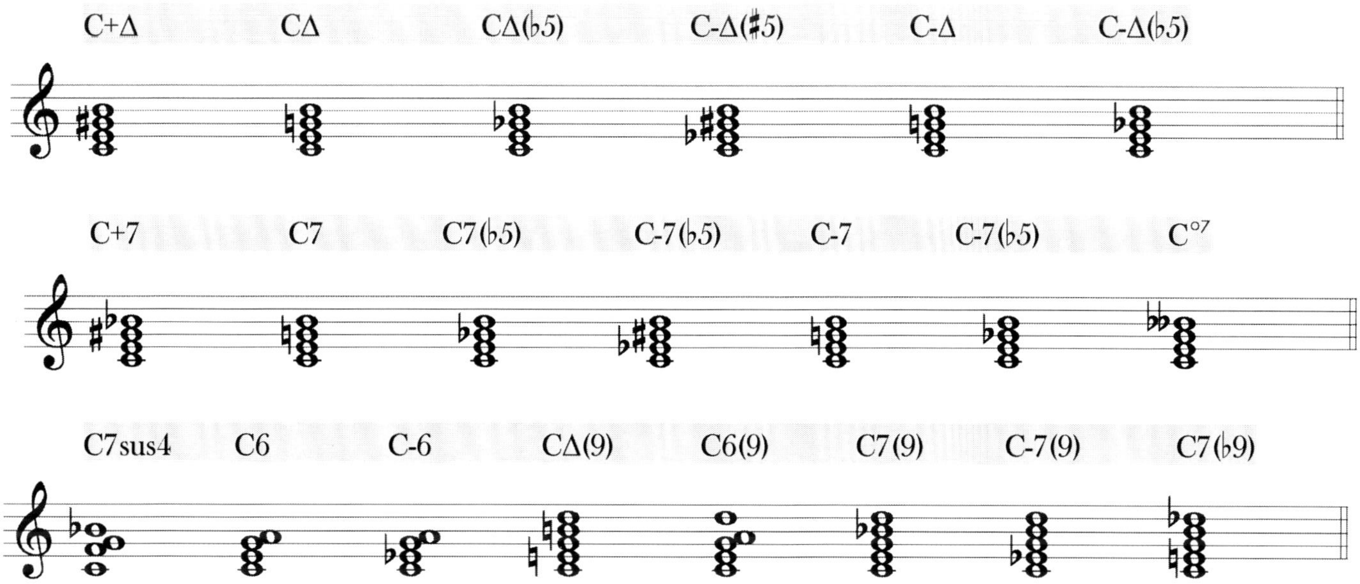

Other alternative notations:
CΔ=Cmaj7=CM7= CΔ7
C-7=Cm7=Cmi7
C-7♭5=C^{ø7} ("half diminished")
C^{o7}=Cdim
C+7=C7+=C7aug=C7aug
C7sus4=C11=B♭/C=G-7/C
C-Δ=Cmin(maj7)=CmΔ=CmΔ7

Chord Symbol Chart

Symbol	Chord Structure	Symbol	Chord Structure
+	1 3 ♯5	6	1 3 5 6
	1 3 5	-6	1 ♭3 5 6
♭5	1 3 ♭5	6(9)	1 3 5 6 9
-	1 ♭3 5	7(♭9)	1 3 5 ♭7 ♭9
o	1 ♭3 ♭5	-Δ(9)	1 ♭3 5 7 9
sus2	1 2 5	-Δ♭5(9)	1 ♭3 ♭5 7 9
sus4	14 5	+7(9)	1 3 ♯5 ♭7 9
sus4(♭5)	1 4 ♭5	+7(♯9)	1 3 ♯5 ♭7 ♯9
sus4(♯5)	1 4 ♯5	7(9)	1 3 5 ♭7 9
Phry	1 ♭2 5	7(♯9)	1 3 5 ♭7 ♯9
Lyd	1 ♯4 5	7♭5(9)	1 3 ♭5 ♭7 9
Lyd ♯5	1 ♯4 ♯5	7♭5(♯9)	1 3 ♭5 ♭7 ♯9
add2	1 2 3 5	-7(9)	1 ♭3 5 ♭7 9
+Δ	1 3 ♯5 7	-7♭5(9)	1 ♭3 ♭5 ♭7 9
Δ	1 3 5 7	Δ(♯11)	1 3 5 7 ♯11
Δ♭5	1 3 ♭5 7	-Δ(♯11)	1 3 5 7 ♯11
-Δ♯5	1 ♭3 ♯5 7	7(♯11)	1 3 5 ♭7 ♯11
-Δ	1 ♭3 5 7	-7(♯11)	1 ♭3 5 ♭7 ♯11
-Δ♭5	1 ♭3 ♭5 7	Δ(♭13)	1 3 5 7 ♭13
+7	1 3 ♯5 ♭7	-Δ(♭13)	1 ♭3 5 7 ♭13
7	1 3 5 ♭7	7(♭13)	1 3 5 ♭7 ♭13
7♭5	1 3 ♭5 ♭7	-7(♭13)	1 ♭3 5 ♭7 ♭13
-7♯5	1 ♭3 ♯5 ♭7	Δ♭5(♭13)	1 3 ♭5 7 ♭13
-7	1 ♭3 5 ♭7	7♭5(♭13)	1 3 ♭5 ♭7 ♭13
-7♭5	1 ♭3 ♭5 ♭7	-7♭5(♭13)	1 ♭3 ♭5 ♭7 ♭13
o7	1 3 ♭5 ♭♭7	Δ(♯9,♯11)	1 3 5 7 ♯9 ♯11
6(♭5)	1 3 ♭5 6	Δ(♯9,11)	1 3 5 7 ♯9 11
+Δsus2	1 2 ♯5 7	-Δ(9,♯11)	1 ♭3 5 7 9 ♯11
Δsus2	1 2 5 7	-Δ(9,11)	1 ♭3 5 7 9 11
Δ♭5sus2	1 2 ♭5 7	7♭5(9, 11)	1 3 ♭5 ♭7 9 11
7sus4	1 4 5 ♭7	Δ(9,♯11,♯13)	1 3 5 7 9 ♯11 ♯13
+Δsus4	1 4 ♯5 7	Δ(♯9,♯11,♯13)	1 3 5 7 ♯9 ♯11 ♯13
Δsus4	1 4 5 7	+Δ(9,♯11,♯13)	1 3 ♯5 7 9 ♯11 ♯13
7sus4(♭5)	1 4 ♭5 ♭7	+Δ(♯9,♯11,♯13)	1 3 ♯5 7 ♯9 ♯11 ♯13
+7sus4	1 4 ♯5 ♭7	-Δ(9,♯11,♯13)	1 ♭3 5 7 9 ♯11 ♯13
+7sus2	1 2 ♯5 ♭7	Δ(♭9,11,13)	1 3 5 7 ♭9 11 13
7sus2	1 2 5 ♭7	Δ(♯9,11,13)	1 3 5 7 ♯9 11 13
7♭5sus2	1 2 ♭5 ♭7	7♭5(♭9,11,♭13)	1 3 ♭5 ♭7 ♭9 11 ♭13
+Δ(9)	1 3 ♯5 7 9	7sus4(♭5,9,13)	1 4 ♭5 ♭7 9 13
+Δ(♯9)	1 3 ♯5 7 ♯9	7sus4(♭5,♭9,13)	1 4 ♭5 ♭7 ♭9 13
Δ(9)	1 3 5 7 9	7sus4(♭5,9,♭13)	1 4 ♭5 ♭7 9 ♭13
Δ(♯9)	1 3 5 7 ♯9	7sus4(♭5,♭9,♭13)	1 4 ♭5 ♭7 ♭9 ♭13
Δ♭5(9)	1 3 ♭5 7 9	Δsus4(♯5,♭9,13)	1 4 ♯5 7 ♭9 13
Δ♭5(♯9)	1 3 ♭5 7 ♯9	Δsus4(♯5,9,13)	1 4 ♯5 7 9 13
-Δ♯5(9)	1 ♭3 ♯5 7 9	Δsus4(♯5,♭9,♭13)	1 4 ♯5 7 ♭9 ♭13
-Δ♯5(♯9)	1 ♭3 ♯5 7 ♯9	Δsus4(♯5,9,♭13)	1 4 ♯5 7 9 ♭13

Preface

I began studying the double-symmetrical augmented scale when I was fifteen years old, without even being aware of it. At that time, I was taking guitar lessons from my uncle, who always encouraged me to listen to his favorite musicians. He introduced me to Allan Holdsworth's music, namely to his album *Wardenclyffe Tower*. When I heard Holdsworth's guitar for the first time, I was amazed by both his playing and the "new" sounds reaching my ears. It was astonishing. I realized right then and there that I wanted to know more about him. Later on, I embarked on a thorough study of music theory, hoping that someday I'd be able to understand Holdsworth's music.

Some years later, I attended Berklee College of Music, where I took lessons from Ed Tomassi, Dave Santoro and Tim Miller, among others. It was thanks to my teachers' inspiring classes that I discovered one of the most important secrets of Allan Holdsworth's music: the double-symmetrical augmented scale. They also introduced me to other musicians who favored this scale, such as Mark Turner, Gary Thomas, Nelson Veras, and Jerry Bergonzi.

After studying at Berklee, I decided to dig deeper into the underlying concepts and theory behind "the scale." Unfortunately, this information was hard to come by, since barely anything had ever been published about it. This is what pushed me to start doing my own research.

This book, *the Double-Symmetrical Augmented Scale for Jazz Improvisation* is the result of eight years of investigative work. In this book, I intend to share my conclusions with you while trying to fill this void in the literature. Furthermore, these pages are my humble tribute to Allan Holdsworth.

Welcome to the beginning of a fascinating journey – enjoy the ride!

Xabier Oró

Introduction

The *double-symmetrical augmented scale* has received many names throughout history. The first evidence of its existence goes back to the Ancient Greeks, who used the term, *genus chromaticum scale.* A variety of denominations can be found later on, such as the *nonatonic scale* or *nine-note symmetrical augmented scale,* among others.

Several composers have claimed to be the first to ever use this scale, each having given it a different name. French composer Olivier Messiaen was one of the most successful among them. He called it *Mode 3* in his classification of limited transposition modes (*The Technique of My Musical Language,* 1944).

Russian composer Nicolas Slonimsky, on the other hand, named it the *Tcherepnin scale* in his *Thesaurus of Scales and Melodic Patterns* (1947), honoring his colleague, Alexander Tcherepnin. Eventually, Tcherepnin himself published *Basic Elements of My Musical Language* (1962), where he called it the *nonatonic scale.*

It is worth noting that Slonimsky's thesaurus is a highly systematic compilation of templates which significantly influenced composers and improvisers across genres, including John Coltrane, Allan Holdsworth, and Frank Zappa. Coltrane's bandmate McCoy Tyner — one of the best jazz pianists of all time — said: "Coltrane carried the book with him constantly during the years 1957 to 1959. He always took it with him when he traveled on concert tours, and practiced it as part of his daily routine." Coltrane's in-depth studies of Slonimsky's thesaurus had an undeniable influence on *Giant Steps* (1960), a legendary recording that would change jazz history forever.

Scale Construction

The double-symmetrical augmented scale is a nine-note symmetrical scale. This means that it can be divided into three note groups, each one of them containing three notes which are separated by identical intervals: a major second followed by two minor seconds in an ascending pattern.

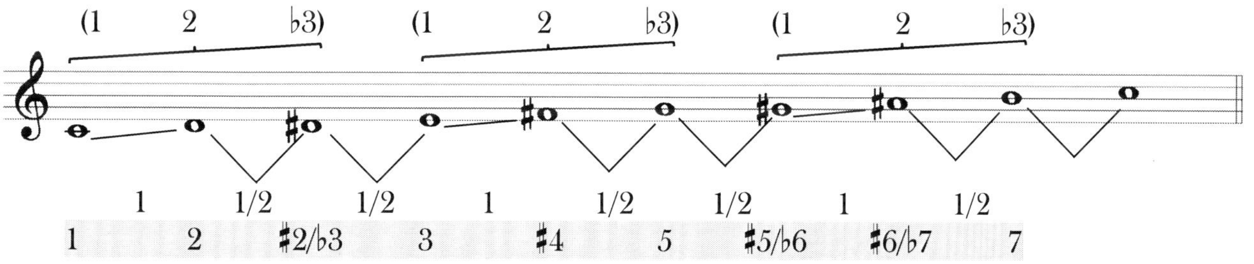

The following scale is a combination of two hexatonic symmetrical augmented scales (1, ♯2/♭3, 3, 5, ♯5/♭6, 7) that contains repeated notes:

C symmetrical augmented scale + B symmetrical augmented scale

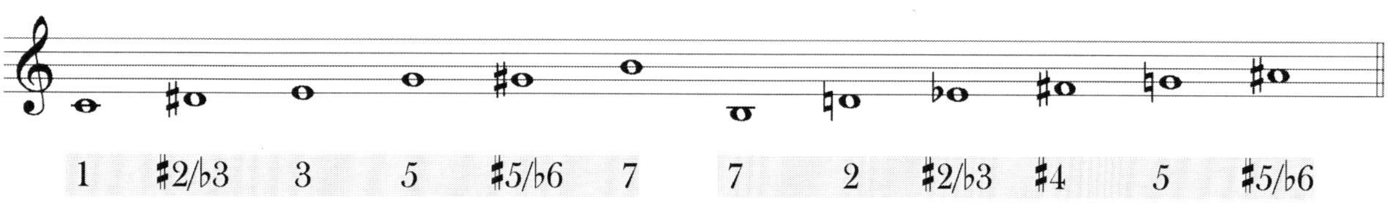

This is why we call it the *double-symmetrical augmented scale.*

We could also see this scale as three augmented triads starting a half step away from each other: C+/B+/B♭+.

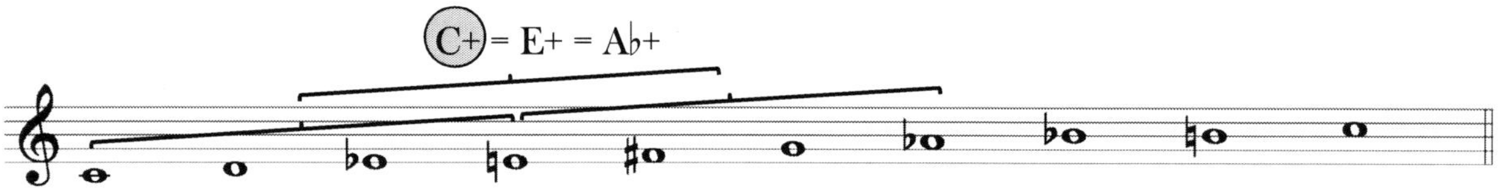

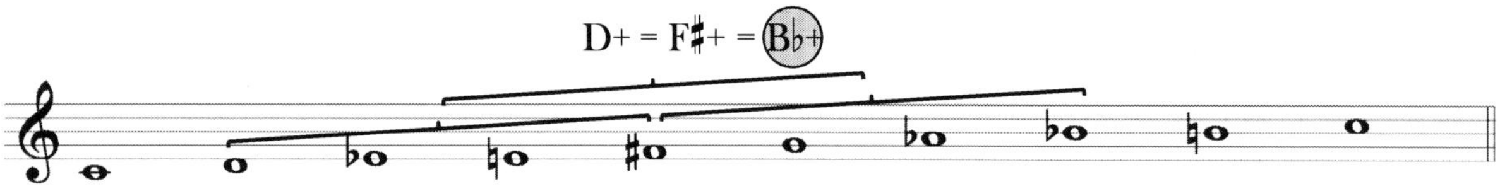

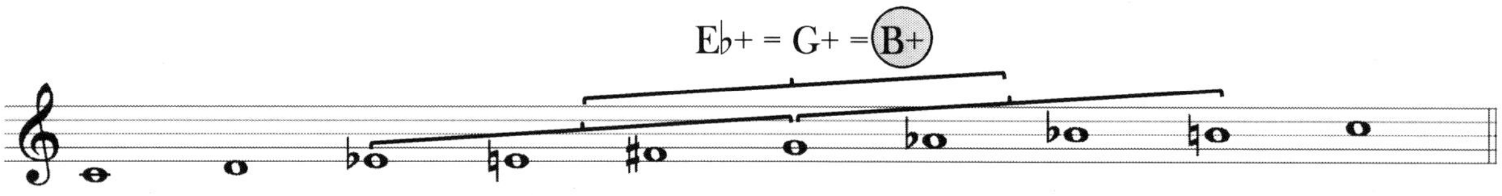

At the same time, this augmented triad pattern repeats itself every major third:

C+ (C E A♭) follows the same pattern as E+ (E A♭ C) and A♭+ (A♭ C E).

This also means that the entire pattern of the double-symmetrical augmented scale repeats itself every major third:

C double-symmetrical augmented = E double-symmetrical augmented = A♭ double-symmetrical augmented

This, in turn, implies that each double-symmetrical augmented scale simultaneously belongs to three keys or tonalities. Consequently, there are only four different double-symmetrical augmented scales in all twelve keys:

12 keys / 3 keys per scale = 4 transpositions.

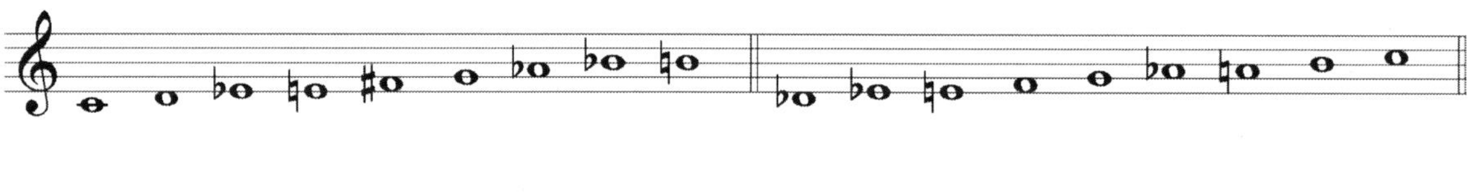

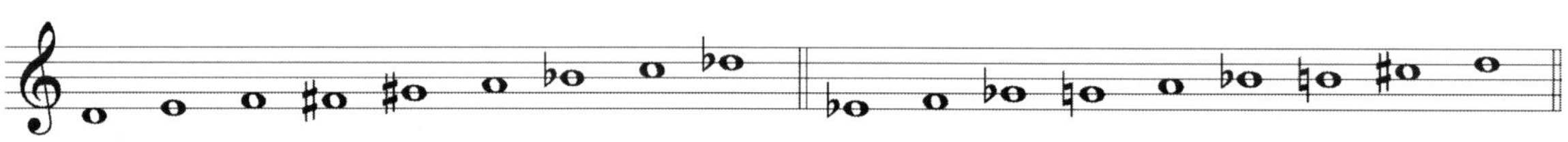

The scale has three modes:

Mode 1 (C whh*)

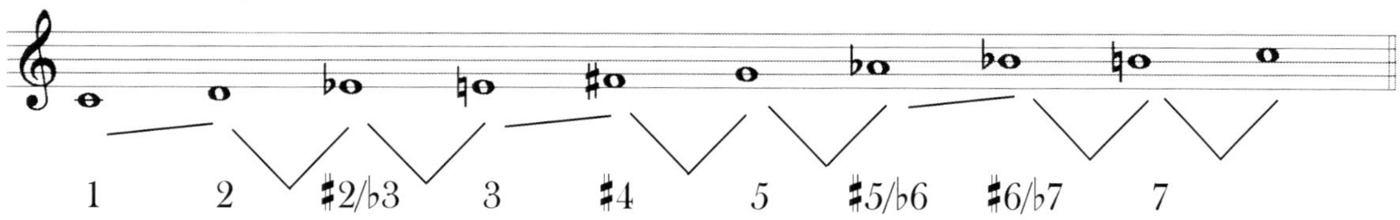

Mode 2 (D hhw)

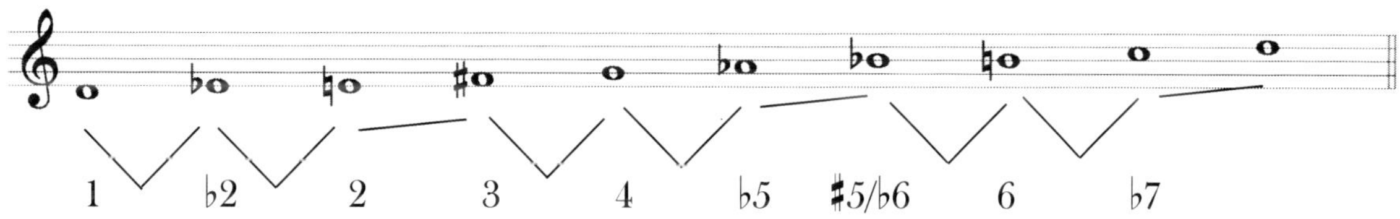

Mode 3 (B hwh)

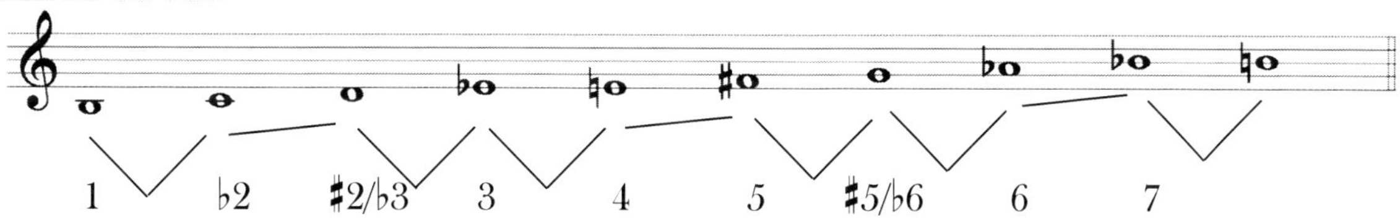

These modes will be analyzed extensively in chapter III.

Next, let's see how some of the aforementioned musicians approached the double-symmetrical augmented scale.

The Olivier Messiaen Approach

Olivier Messiaen included the double-symmetrical augmented scale as the "third mode" of his seven modes of limited transposition (*The Technique of My Musical Language*, 1944):

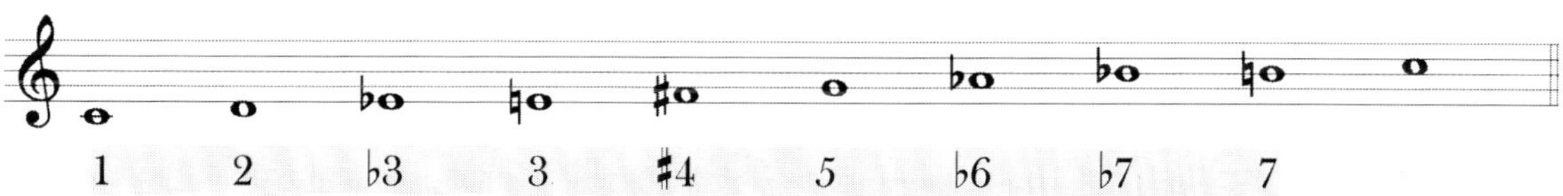

These modes are very prominent in Messiaen's work. This can be explained by his fascination with what he called the "charm of impossibilities" in music.

Messiaen realized that, except for E♭, all other notes in this scale matched the fourth octave of the overtone series.

**w= whole step, h=half step*

Here's the overtone series:

1st Octave 2nd Octave 3rd Octave 4th Octave

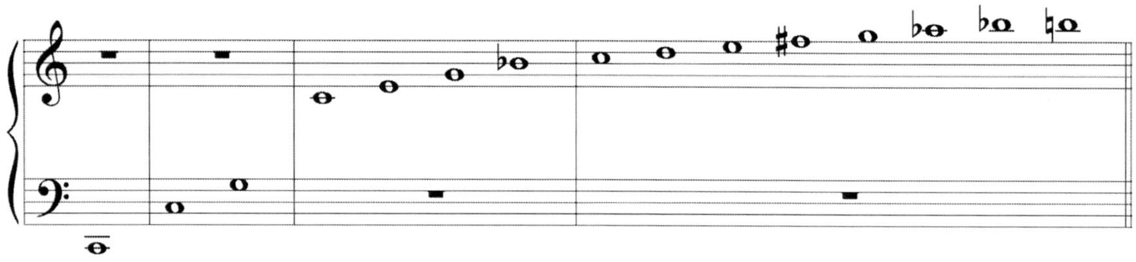

1 1 5 1 3 5 ♭7 1 2 3 ♯4 5 ♭6 ♭7 7

Messiaen utilized this phenomenon to create the *resonance chord,* which can be heard in his celebrated *Quartet for the End of Time.* The resonance chord is a polychord featuring a C7 in the lower octave (1 3 5 ♭7, like the third octave of the overtone series) and a B-6/D in the upper octave (2 ♯4 ♯5 7, the remaining notes in the double-symmetrical augmented scale).

B-6/D over C7 — B-6/D add (E♭) over C7

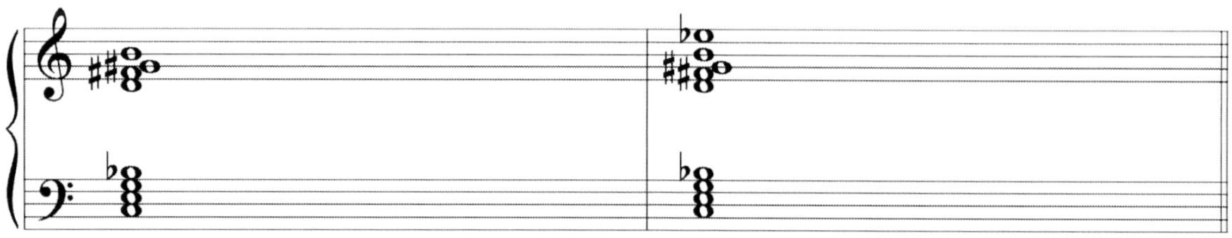

As you can see, the second chord in the example above is a *resonance chord with an added E♭*, rendering the complete double-symmetrical augmented scale.

The Alexander Tcherepnin Approach

Alexander Tcherepnin found the Tcherepnin (nonatonic) scale by combining two, six-note (hexatonic) augmented scales:

The first hexatonic augmented scale was the result of overlapping minor and major 3rds in an ascending pattern.

C hexatonic augmented scale: C E♭ E G G♯ B C

The second hexatonic augmented scale was the result of overlapping minor and major 3rds in a descending pattern.

D♭ hexatonic augmented scale: D♭ E F A♭ A C D♭

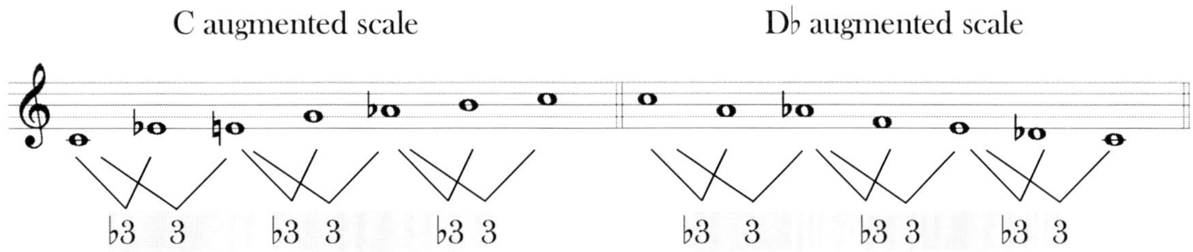

Combining both scales produce the C Tcherepnin or nonatonic scale (NON):

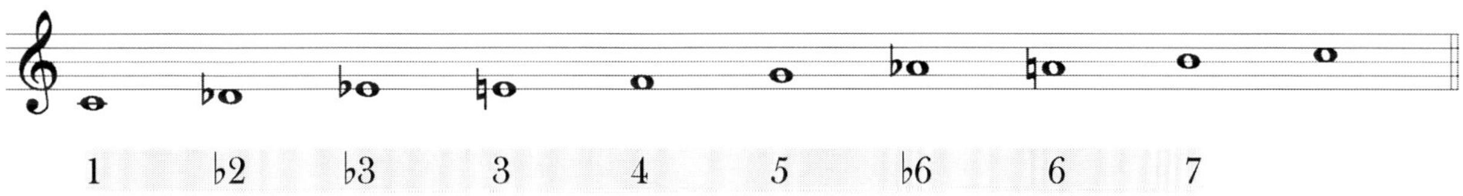

At a glance, the Tcherepnin scale looks different from Messiaen's mode 3. This is only because the Tcherepnin scale starts from a different note or mode:

The second mode of the Tcherepnin scale is identical to the first mode of Messiaen's mode 3 scale.

B Tcherepnin Scale:

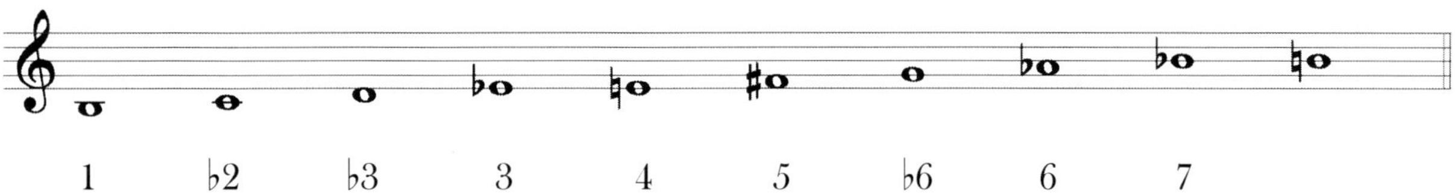

The second mode of the B Tcherepnin scale = C Messiaen's mode 3 scale

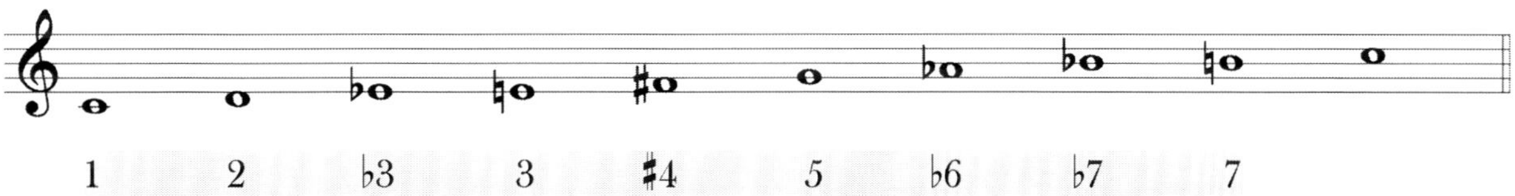

The Nicolas Slonimsky Approach

Slonimsky found the double-symmetrical augmented scale by first creating what he called a *ditone progression* (adding two equal distance notes between an octave or dividing one octave into three equal parts). The process described below can be found in his *Thesaurus of Scales and Melodic Patterns*.

The Ditone Progression:

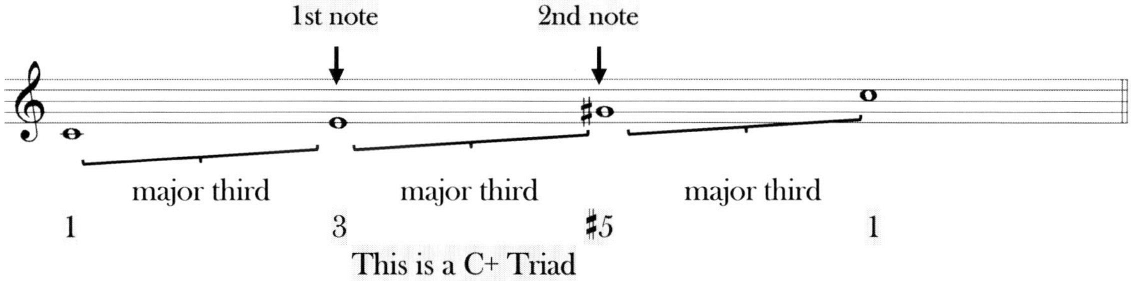

Then, he applied an *interpolation of two notes* (double chromatics) to the augmented triad. By approaching each note of the triad with double chromatics, he identified the three modes of the double-symmetrical augmented scale (see below).

The Tcherepnin scale (example 184 in the *Thesaurus*):

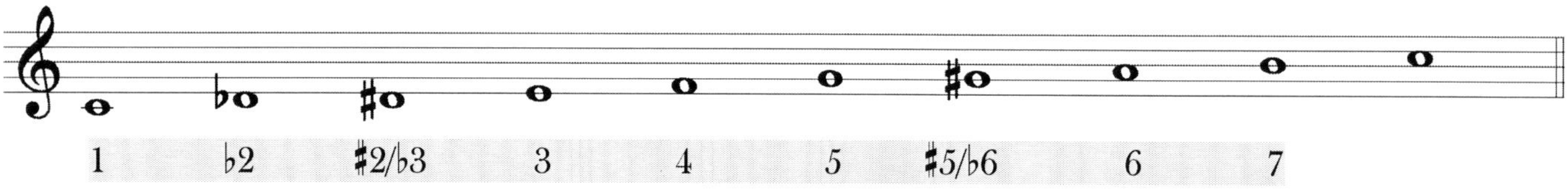

An equivalent to Messiaen's mode 3 (Example 185 in the *Thesaurus*):

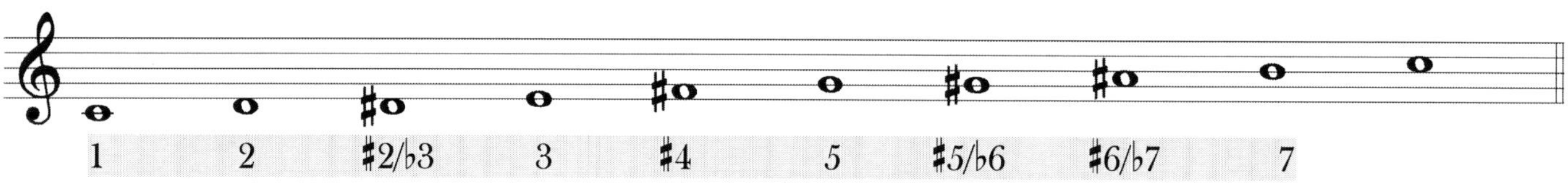

Mode 2 of the double-symmetrical augmented scale, as explained later in this book (Example 183 in the *Thesaurus*):

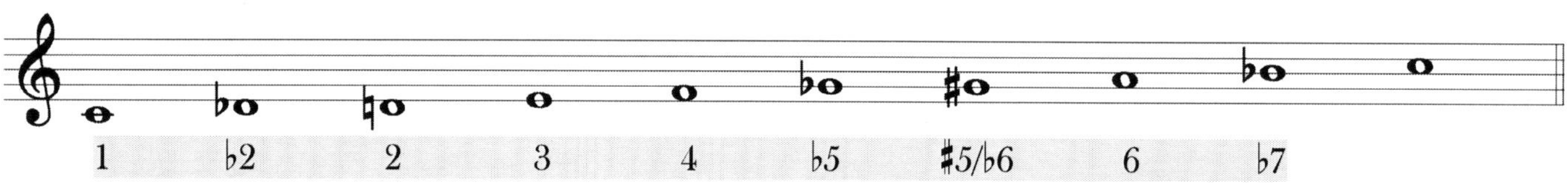

The John Coltrane Approach

"By 1951 or 1952, John Coltrane was familiar with Nicholas Slonimsky's *Thesaurus of Scales and Melodic Patterns* which he had learned about from his theory teacher Dennis Sandole, who was interested in scalar approaches to music."

J. Collier, *The Making of Jazz: A Comprehensive History* (1978).

As I mentioned earlier, musicians like McCoy Tyner or Wayne Shorter have stated that Coltrane obsessively studied Slonimsky's *Thesaurus of scales and Melodic Patterns* for years. Therefore, it's no surprise that many of Slonimsky's concepts can be heard in Coltrane's music.

In his tune "Giant Steps," Coltrane divided the key of B major into three equal parts (ditone progression): B major, E♭ major, and G major. This concept has a direct connection to Slonimsky, since it is exactly the same process explained in his *Thesaurus.*

Below is a composition based on the chord changes in "Giant Steps," which I've named "Augmented Steps."

Augmented Steps

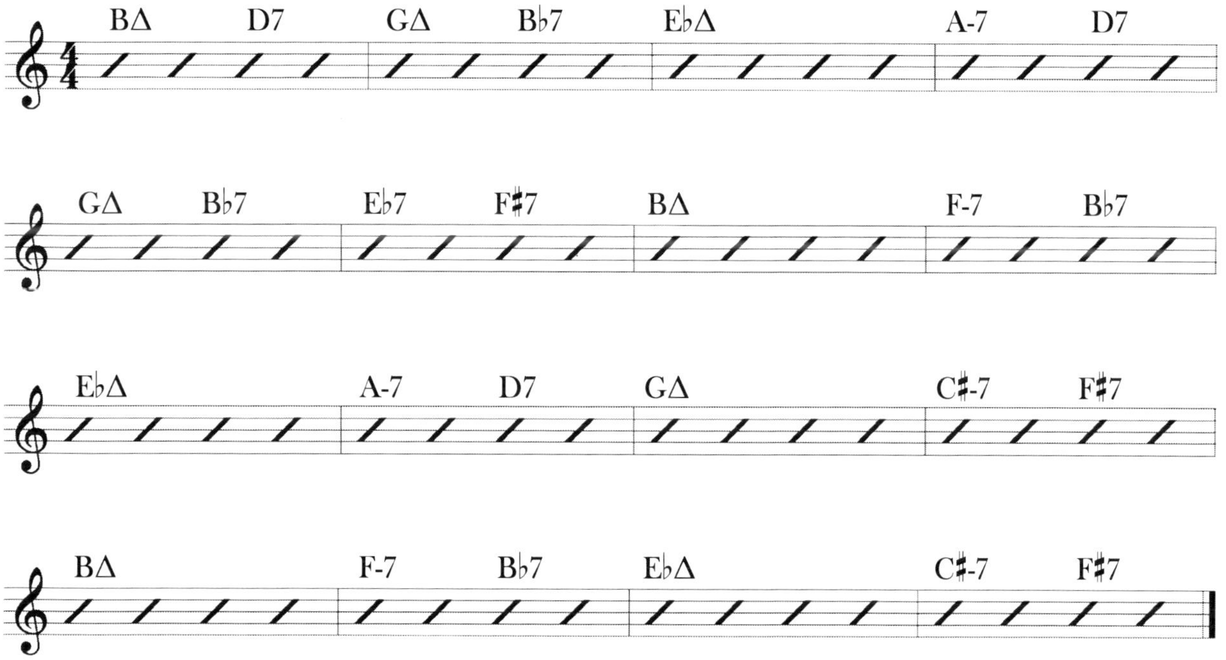

This composition starts in B major (BΔ), modulates to G major via its dominant chord (D7), then modulates to E♭ major via its dominant chord (B♭7), and finally modulates to GΔ via a II-7 V7 (A-7 D7) change, restarting the same chord cycle in the new key.

Coltrane used these cycles to reharmonize standards, as well as to improvise and superimpose melodic lines over other chord changes, producing an in/out effect.

Let's take a look at the chord roots in "Augmented Steps," organized by type:

Chord type	Chord Roots		
Δ	B	E♭	G
7	D	F♯	B♭
-7	A	C♯	F

Next, let's arrange them starting from B:

B C♯ D D♯ F F♯ G A B♭

Surprise!

We get the B double-symmetrical augmented scale:

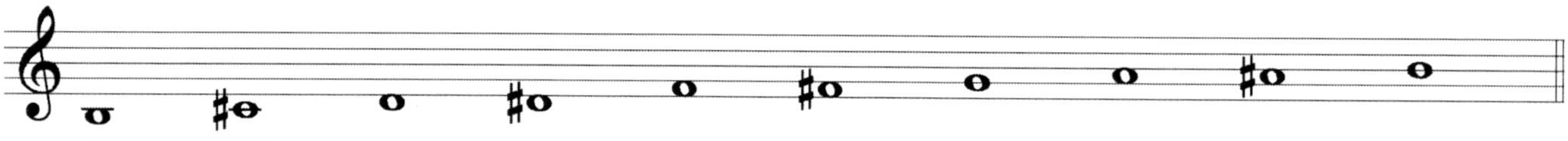

1 2 ♯2/♭3 3 ♯4 5 ♯5/♭6 ♯6/♭7 7

This is the diatonic scale of "Giant Steps"!

And now, let's pay attention to the original melody in "Giant Steps."

If we divide the composition in 4-bar groups and organize the notes based on which group they belong to, we come up with something like this:

Bars	Melody Notes						
Bars 1-4	F♯	D	B	G	B♭	B	A
Bars 5-8	D	B♭	G	D♯	F♯	G	F
Bars 9-12	B♭	B	A	D	D♯	C♯	
Bars 13-16	F♯	F♯	G	F	B♭	F♯	F♯

Next, let's arrange the melody notes starting from B:

B C♯ D D♯ F F♯ G A B♭ B

And here it is again! The B double-symmetrical augmented scale.

But wait, there's yet another interesting detail I'd like to share with you... If we apply Coltrane's famous pattern 1 2 3 5 to the three tonal centers in "Giant Steps," we get the following:

B add2 (4-note grouping) G add2 E♭ add2

1 2 3 5 1 2 3 5 1 2 3 5

If we then reorganize these same notes as a scale, we find once again, you guessed it: the B double-symmetrical augmented scale.

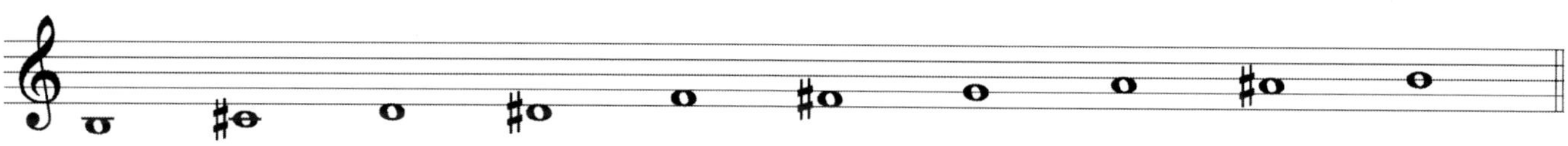

1 2 ♯2/♭3 3 ♯4 5 ♯5/♭6 ♯6/♭7 7

Was this intentional or just a coincidence? We can't know for sure, but whatever the case may be, the double-symmetrical augmented scale clearly influenced many jazz musicians in successive generations, including: Mark Turner, Allan Holdsworth, Jerry Bergonzi, Gary Thomas, Greg Osby, Nelson Veras, Kurt Rosenwinkel, Jonathan Kreisberg, Melissa Aldana, Tim Miller, Rez Abbasi, Wolfgang Muthspiel, Mike Stern, and many more.

I. How the Double-Symmetrical Augmented Scale Fits in the Tonal System

Let's start by briefly reviewing the major scale:

C Major Scale

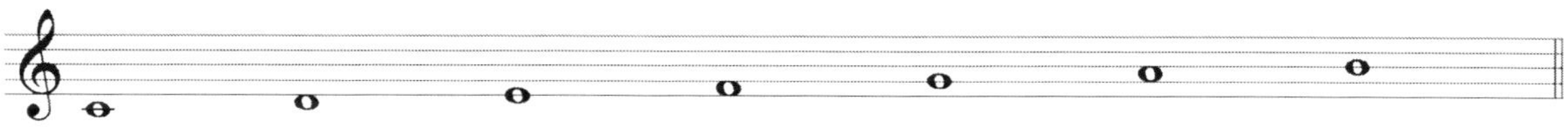

1 2 3 4 5 6 7

If we superimpose thirds on each note of the scale, we get the following chords:

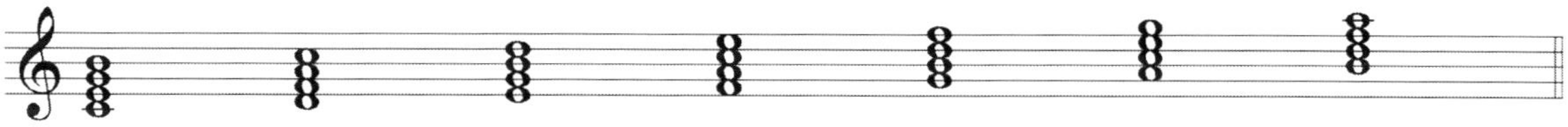

CΔ D-7 E-7 FΔ G7 A-7 B-7(♭5)

By placing the tonic on different degrees of the major scale, we get another six scales. Each of the following scales represents a mode:

Cmajor/C	=	C Ionian	=	1 2 3 4 5 6 7
Cmajor/D	=	D Dorian	=	1 2 ♭3 4 5 6 ♭7
Cmajor/E	=	E Phrygian	=	1 ♭2 ♭3 4 5 ♭6 ♭7
Cmajor/F	=	F Lydian	=	1 2 3 ♯4 5 6 7
Cmajor/G	=	G Mixolydian	=	1 2 3 4 5 6 ♭7
Cmajor/A	=	A Aeolian	=	1 2 ♭3 4 5 ♭6 ♭7
Cmajor/B	=	B Locrian	=	1 ♭2 ♭3 4 ♭5 ♭6 ♭7

Dominant Function

Tonal harmony is based on the idea of tension/resolution between the first and the fifth degree of the major scale: V7 to IΔ. The dominant chord is the most unstable (tense) chord in any major key because it contains the *tritone*. The tritone is a dissonant interval that occurs between the seventh and the fourth degrees (B and F in C major). This interval is found in the chord of the fifth degree (Dominant V7), between its major 3rd and its flat 7th.

These two notes have a strong need to resolve to the notes a half-step away from them. In the key of C, this would be B resolving to C and F resolving to E. The notes C and E represent the one and the third in the first chord of the tonality (I), which is always the most stable chord.

This movement is at the core of the *perfect authentic cadence*, which takes place between the fifth and the first chord of the key.

V7	IΔ
G7	CΔ

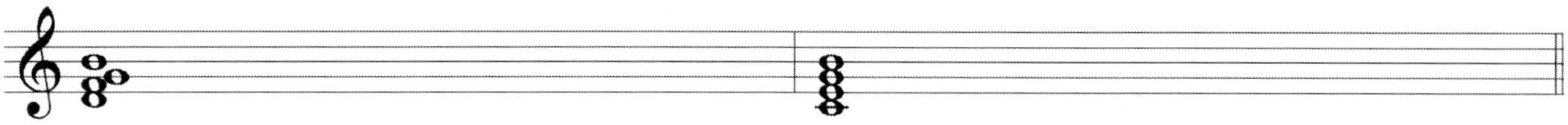

Secondary Dominants

In jazz music it is typical to expand the aforementioned tension/release movement (V-I) to other chords of the major scale, creating secondary dominant chords for each note of the scale.

Secondary dominants expressed as "V7," are followed by a slash and the degree that it would naturally resolve to:

	IΔ	II-7	III-7	IVΔ	V7	VI-7	VII-7♭5
Resolution Chord	CΔ	D-7	E-7	FΔ	G7	A-7	B-7♭5
Secondary Dominants	G7	A7	B7	C7	D7	E7	-*
	V7/I	V7/II	V7/III	V7/IV	V7/V	V7/VI	-*

* Not used because the V7/VII has no diatonic root (that pertains to the original key)

Some secondary dominant chords have a strong relationship with the double-symmetrical augmented scale which we'll observe in this chapter.

V7/ II Melodic Minor

In order to create a secondary dominant chord that resolves to the second degree (V7/II), we can raise the third of an A-7 (Am7) from C to C♯, turning it into an A7 chord, the dominant 7th of D melodic minor. If we build a scale from the root of the target chord, we get a D melodic minor scale. Unlike its use in traditional classical music, the *jazz minor* scale employs the raised 6th and 7th degrees of the melodic minor both ascending and descending.

D melodic minor

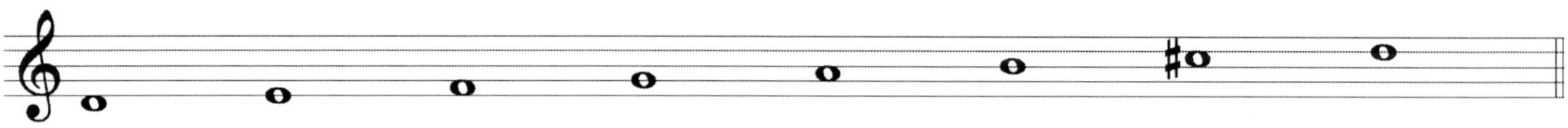

D-Δ	E-7	F+Δ	G7	A7	B-7♭5	C♯-7♭5

Below are the modes of the melodic minor scale compared to the modes of the major scale:

Melodic Minor		Major	
D melodic minor	1 2 ♭3 4 5 6 7	D Dorian	1 2 ♭3 4 5 6 ♭7
E Phrygian ♮6	1 ♭2 ♭3 4 5 6 ♭7	E Phrygian	1 ♭2 ♭3 4 5 ♭6 ♭7
F Lydian ♯5	1 2 3 ♯4 ♯5 6 7	F Lydian	1 2 3 ♯4 5 6 7
G Mixolydian ♯4	1 2 3 ♯ 4 5 6 ♭7	G Mixolydian	1 2 3 4 5 6 ♭7
A Mixolydian ♭6	1 2 3 4 5 ♭6 ♭7	A Aeolian	1 2 ♭3 4 5 ♭6 ♭7
B Locrian ♮2	1 2 ♭3 4 ♭5 ♭6 ♭7	B Locrian	1 ♭2 ♭3 4 ♭5 ♭6 ♭7
C♯ Altered	1 ♭2 ♯2 3 ♯4 ♯5 ♭7	C Ionian	1 2 3 4 5 6 7

V7/III Neapolitan Minor

In order to create a secondary dominant chord that resolves to the third degree (V7/III), we can raise the third of a B-7♭5 (Bm7♭5 or B^{ø7}) from D to D♯, turning it into a B7♭5, the dominant 7th of E Neapolitan minor.

If we build a scale from the root of the target chord, we get an E Neapolitan minor.

E Neapolitan minor

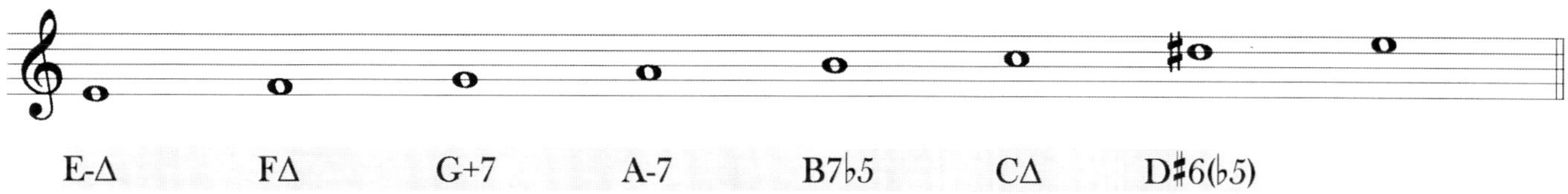

Below are the modes of the Neapolitan minor scale compared to the modes of the major scale:

Neapolitan Minor		Major	
E Neapolitan Minor	1 ♭2 ♭3 4 5 ♭6 7	E Phrygian	1 ♭2 ♭3 4 5 ♭6 ♭7
F Lydian ♯6	1 2 3 ♯4 5 ♯6 7	F Lydian	1 2 3 ♯4 5 6 7
G Mixolydian ♯5	1 2 3 4 ♯5 6 ♭7	G Mixolydian	1 2 3 4 5 6 ♭7
A Aeolian ♯4	1 2 ♭3 ♯4 5 ♭6 ♭7	A Aeolian	1 2 ♭3 4 5 ♭6 ♭7
B Mixolydian ♭5(♭2,♭6)	1 ♭2 3 4 ♭5 ♭6 ♭7	B Locrian	1 ♭2 ♭3 4 ♭5 ♭6 ♭7
C Ionian ♯2	1 ♯2 3 4 5 6 7	C Ionian	1 2 3 4 5 6 7
D♯ Dorian Dim.	1 ♭2 ♭♭3 ♭4 ♭5 ♭6 ♭♭7	D Dorian	1 2 ♭3 4 5 6 ♭7

V7/IV

In order to create a secondary dominant chord that resolves to the fourth degree (V7/IV), of the major scale, we could change the seventh of a CΔ from B to B♭, turning it into a C7. However, this would only result in a modulation to F major, so no new scales would be created.

V7/V

In order to create a secondary dominant chord that resolves to the fifth degree (V7/V), we could shift the third of a D-7=Dm7 from F to F♯, turning it into a D7. However, this would only result in a modulation to G major, so again, no new scales would be created.

V7/VI Harmonic Minor

In order to create a secondary dominant chord that resolves to the sixth degree (V7/VI), we can shift the third of an E-7 (Em7) from G to G♯, turning it into an E7.

If we build a scale from the root of the target chord, we get an A harmonic minor scale:

A harmonic minor

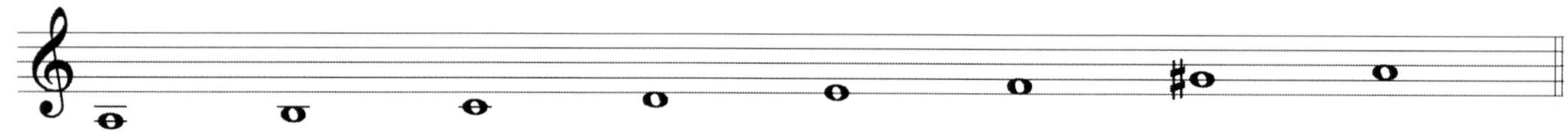

A-Δ B-7♭5 C+Δ D-7 E7 FΔ G♯°7

Below are the modes of the harmonic minor scale versus the modes of the major scale:

Harmonic Minor		Major	
A Harmonic Minor	1 2 ♭3 4 5 ♭6 7	A Aeolian	1 2 ♭3 4 5 ♭6 ♭7
B Locrian ♮6	1 ♭2 ♭3 4 ♭5 6 ♭7	B Locrian	1 ♭2 ♭3 4 ♭5 ♭6 ♭7
C Ionian ♯5	1 2 3 4 ♯5 6 7	C Ionian	1 2 3 4 5 6 7
D Dorian ♯4	1 2 ♭3 ♯4 5 6 ♭7	D Dorian	1 2 ♭3 4 5 6 ♭7
E Mixolydian ♭2, ♭6	1 ♭2 3 4 5 ♭6 ♭7	E Phrygian	1 ♭2 ♭3 4 5 ♭6 ♭7
F Lydian ♯2	1 ♯2 3 ♯4 5 6 7	F Lydian	1 2 3 ♯4 5 6 7
G♯Altered ♭♭7	1 ♭2 ♭3 ♭4 ♭5 ♭6 ♭♭7	G Mixolydian	1 2 3 4 5 6 ♭7

V7/VII

The bass note in this secondary dominant chord would be non-diatonic, that is, it would not belong to the original key. Therefore, this variation is not useful for analytical purposes.

The Double-Symmetrical Augmented Scale

If you look closely, you'll notice that all three scales created from secondary dominants (V7/II, V7/III, V7/VI) contain an augmented triad:

a) V7/II (D melodic minor)

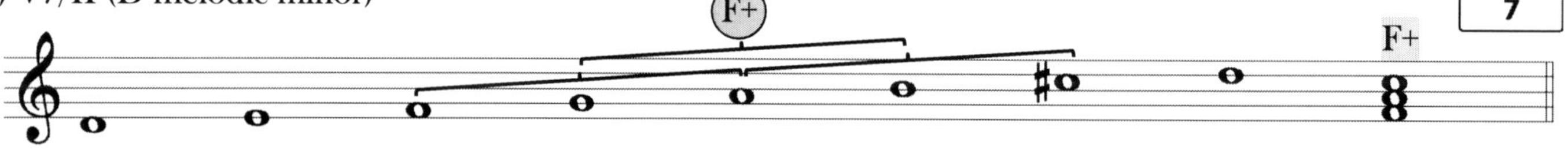

D-Δ E-7 F+Δ G7 A7 B-7♭5 C♯-7♭5

Augmented triad: F+= F A C♯

b) V7/III (E Neapolitan minor)

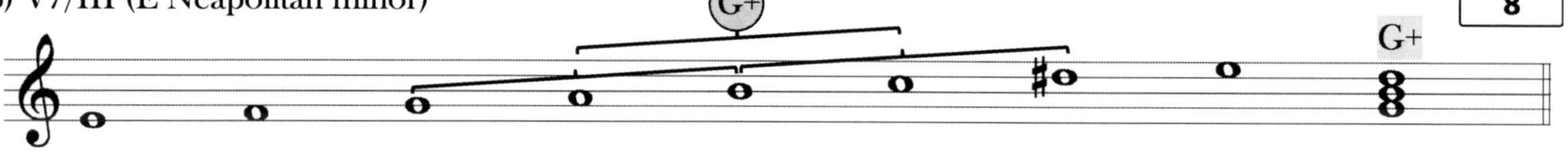

E-Δ FΔ G+7 A-7 B7♭5 CΔ D♯6(♭5)

Augmented triad: G+= G B D♯

c) V7/VI (A harmonic minor)

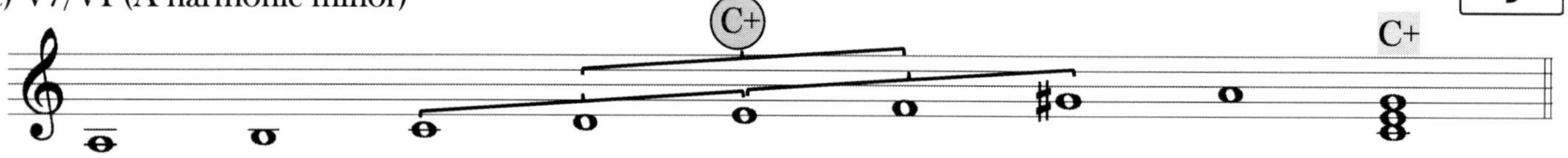

A-Δ B-7♭5 C+Δ D-7 E7 FΔ G♯°7

Augmented triad: C+= C E G♯

Below is the result of combining all three augmented triads (F+, G+, C+) into a single scale:

F			A			C♯		
	G			B			D♯	
		G♯			C			E
F	G	G♯	A	B	C	C♯	D♯	E

And voilà, here it is!

The F double-symmetrical augmented scale! = **F G G♯ A B C C♯ D♯ E**
1 2 ♯2 3 ♯4 5 ♯5 ♯6 7

10

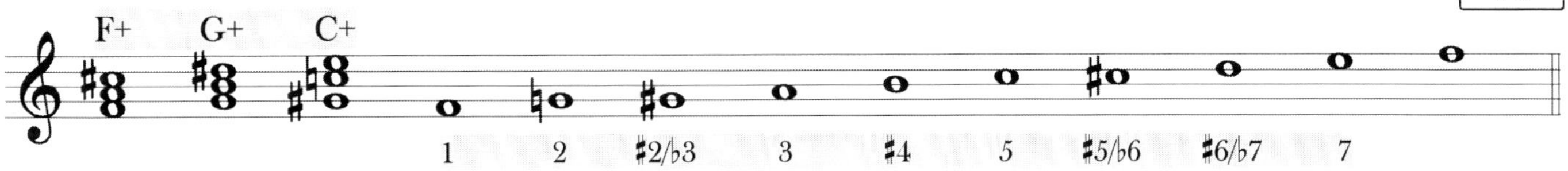

The double-symmetrical augmented scale is a Lydian scale, minus the 6th degree, plus the three notes generating the secondary dominant chords we just saw:

G♯ generates the A harmonic minor.
C♯ generates the D melodic minor.
D♯ generates the E Neapolitan minor.

Consequently, the double-symmetrical augmented scale travels in and out of parallel modal interchanges or intratonal harmonic systems connected to the original key. This differs from other symmetrical scales that actually modulate to other keys, like the diminished symmetrical scale.

C Major	(Lydian)=	FΔ	G7	A-7	B-7♭5	CΔ	D-7	E-7
D Melodic Minor	(Lydian ♯5)=	F+Δ	G7	A7	B-7♭5	C♯-7♭5	D-Δ	E-7
E Neapolitan Minor	(Lydian ♯6)=	FΔ	G+7	A-7	B7♭5	CΔ	D♯6(♭5)	E-Δ
A Harmonic Minor	(Lydian ♯2)=	FΔ	G♯°7	A-Δ	B-7♭5	C+Δ	D-7	E7

In conclusion, the **F double-symmetrical augmented scale** is the scale used in **C major/A minor**, A harmonic minor, D melodic minor and E Neapolitan minor. (See more information in chapter IV.)

The notes generating secondary dominant chords (G♯, C♯, D♯) and the tonics of the secondary dominant chords themselves (E, A, B) create two sus4 chords (Esus4, G♯sus4). The rest of the notes needed to complete an F double-symmetrical augmented scale are C, F and G, which create a third Csus4 chord. Therefore, we could organize all the notes of the scale into three sus4 chords (or their sus2 inversions) separated by major thirds, as shown below:

11

II. Modes of the Double-Symmetrical Augmented Scale

Having a good comprehension of the modes of the double-symmetrical scale is essential for creating an understandable improvisational line and composing interesting chord progressions with the scale. As we've already seen, the double-symmetrical augmented scale has three modes that repeat themselves every major 3rd:

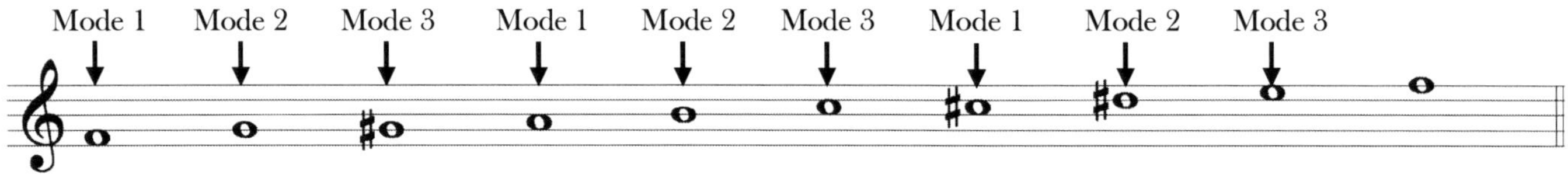

In this chapter, we'll dive deeper into the main features of each mode.

Mode 1

The first mode is the F, A, or C♯ double-symmetrical augmented scale or whh (whole-half-half)

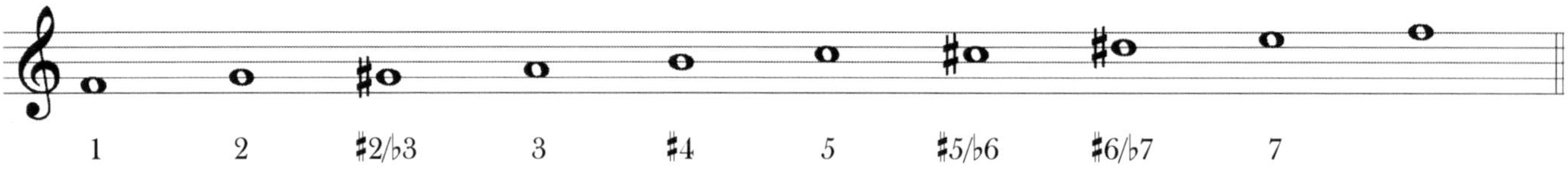

F G G♯ A B C D♭ D♯ E
1 2 ♯2 3 ♯4 5 ♭6 ♯6 7

Mode 1 produces the following chord:

FΔ (9,♯9,♯11,♭13,♯13)

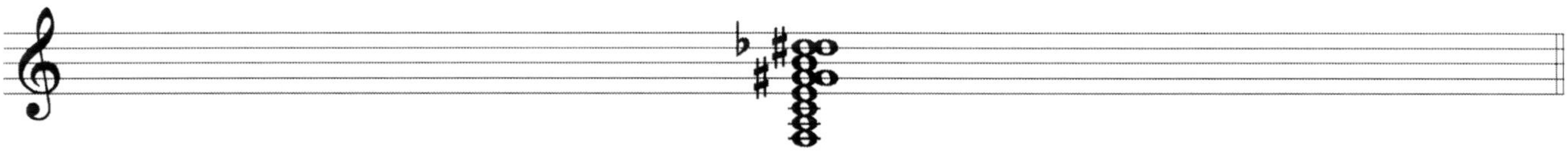

You can see this mode as a Lydian ♭6 add (♯2, ♯6). Another option could be an F harmonic major ♯4 add (♯2, ♯6). This mode could also be called the *F nine-note augmented scale*, *F Messiaen mode 3*, or *F nonatonic scale.*

Mode 2

The second mode is the G, B, or D♯ hhw (half-half-whole) or dominant double-symmetrical augmented scale.

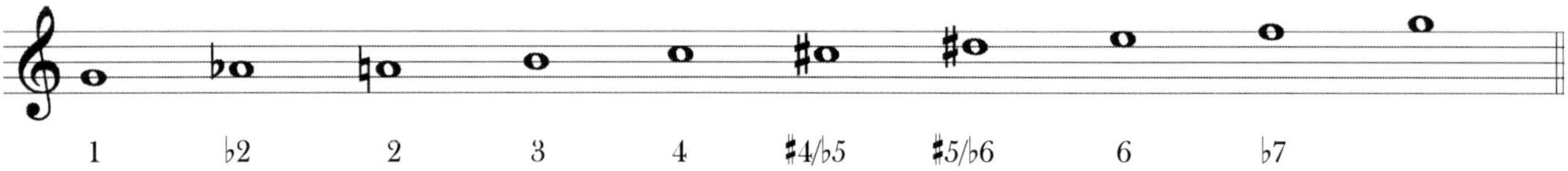

G A♭ A B C C♯ D♯ E F
1 ♭2 2 3 4 ♯4 ♯5 6 ♭7

Mode 2 produces the following chord:

G7♭5 (♭9, 9, 11,♭13, 13)

You can see this mode as a Mixolydian ♭5 add (♭2, ♭6) or a Mixolydian ♯5 add (♭2,♯4).

Mode 3

The third mode is the E, G♯, or C hwh (half-whole-half) or tonic double-symmetrical augmented scale.

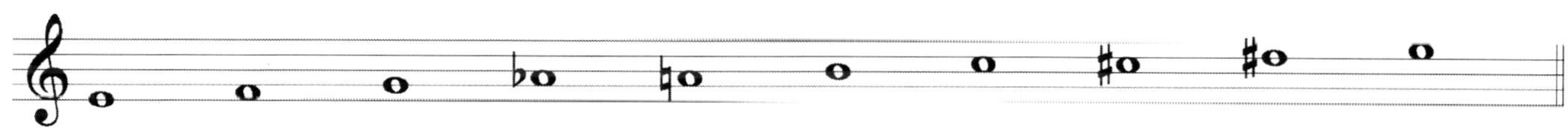

1 ♭2 ♯2/♭3 3 4 5 ♯5/♭6 6 7

E F G G♯ A B C C♯ D♯
1 ♭2 ♯2 3 4 5 ♭6 6 7

Mode 3 produces the following chord:

EΔ (♭9, ♯9, 11, ♭13, 13)

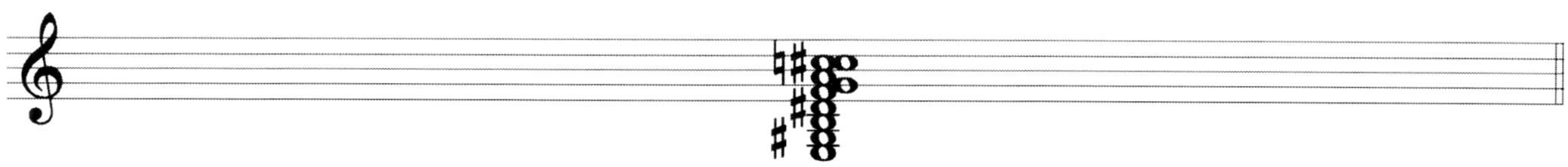

You can see this mode as a Phrygian major (♯2, 6) or an Ionian ♭2 add (♯2, ♭6). It can also be called the *Tcherepnin scale.*
As a result, the modes of the double-symmetrical augmented scale can be summarized as follows:

Modes of the Double-Symmetrical Augmented Scale	
Mode 1	(FΔ, AΔ, C♯Δ) whh Or double-symmetrical augmented
Mode 2	(G7♭5, B7♭5, D♯7♭5) hhw
Mode 3	(CΔ, EΔ, G♯Δ) hwh

Mode 1

The Double-Symmetrical Augmented Whole-Half-Half Scale

Lydian ♭6 add (♯2, ♯6)

Messiaen M3

The double-symmetrical augmented scale consists of a whole step followed by two half steps in an ascending pattern. (whh).

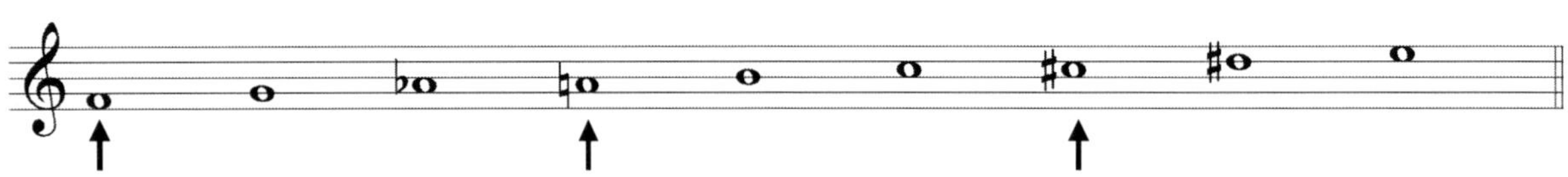

Mode 1: FΔ(9,♯9, ♯11,♭13,♯13) AΔ(9,♯9, ♯11,♭13,♯13) C♯Δ(9,♯9, ♯11,♭13,♯13)

You can see it as a Lydian ♭6 add (♯2, ♯6).

F G G♯ A B C D♭ D♯ E
1 2 ♯2 3 ♯4 5 ♭6 ♯6 7

The first, fourth and seventh degree of the scale create a major 7th chord with a natural 9th, a sharp 9th, a sharp 11th, a flatted 13th, and a sharp 13th as extensions.

Chord:

FΔ (9, ♯9, ♯11, ♭13, ♯13)

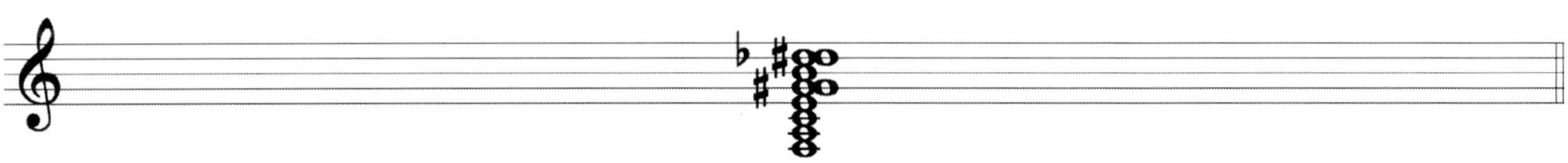

Let's examine the scale with different textures:

1) Two-Note Texture:

This mode features eight intervals: 2, ♯2 or ♭3, 3, ♯4, 5, ♭6, ♯6 or ♭7, and 7.

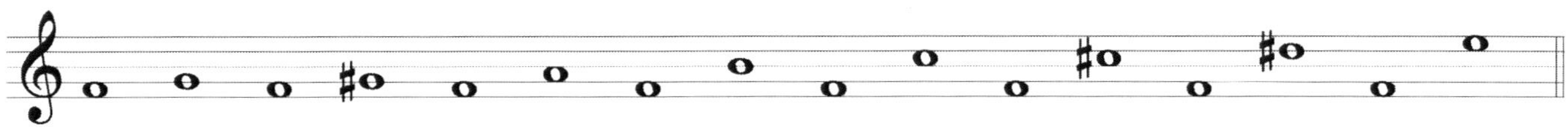

2) Three-Note Texture:

2.1) Triads

There are five kinds of triads in the 1st, 4th and 7th degrees of the scale.

Triads
F+
F
F-
Fo
Fsus2

2.2) Trichords

A trichord is a contiguous 3-note set of distinct pitches within a larger grouping system of three. Here are some of the most common trichords:

1 3 7	1 5 7	1 4 5	Cluster
FΔ no 5	F+Δ no 3	F Lyd (1 ♯4 5)	1 2 ♭3
F-Δ no 5	FΔ no 3	F+ Lyd	1 2 3
F7 no 5	FΔ♭5 no 3		1 ♯2 3
F-7 no 5	F+7 no 3		
	F7 no 3		
	F7♭5 no 3		

3) Four-Note Texture:

3.1) Four-Note Chords

Chords
F+Δ
FΔ
FΔ♭5
F-Δ♯5
F-Δ
F-Δ♭5
F+7
F7
F7♭5
F-7♯5
F-7
F-7♭5
F+Δsus2
FΔsus2
FΔ♭5sus2
F+7sus2
F7sus2
F7♭5sus2

3.2) Melodic Structures

Melodic structures are four-note groupings based on Coltrane's patterns 1 2 3 5 and 1 ♭3 4 5. Below are some options:

Melodic Structures	
1 2 3 5	1 2 ♭3 ♯5
1 2 3 ♯5	1 2 ♭3 ♭5
1 2 3 ♭5	1 ♭3 ♯4 5
1 ♯2 3 5	1 ♭3 ♯4 ♯5
1 ♯2 3 ♯5	1 3 ♯4 5
1 ♯2 3 ♭5	1 3 ♯4 ♯5
1 2 ♭3 5	

3.3) Trichords with Added Notes

1 3 7	1 5 7	1 4 5	Cluster
FΔ no 5 add ♯2	F+Δ no3 add 5	Fsus♯4 add5	F G A♭ A
FΔ no 5 add ♯6	F+Δ no3 add ♭5	F+sus♯4 add5	
	F+Δ no3 add ♯6	Fsus♯4 add♯5	
	FΔ no3 add ♭5		
	FΔ no3 add♯6		
	FΔ♭5 no3 add♯6		

4) Five-Note Texture: Pentatonics

In this case, pentatonics are any five-note combination. Here are some possibilities:

Pentatonics	
1 2 3 5 ♭6	1 2 ♯2 3 ♯5
1 ♯2 3 5 ♭6	1 3 ♯4 5 7
1 2 3 ♭5 ♭6	1 3 ♯4 5 ♭7
1 ♯2 3 ♭5 ♭6	1 3 ♯4 ♯5 7
1 2 3 5 ♭7	1 3 ♯4 ♯5 ♭7
1 ♯2 3 5 ♭7	1 ♭3 ♯4 5 7
1 2 3 ♭5 ♭7	1 ♭3 ♯4 5 ♭7
1 ♯2 3 ♭5 ♭7	1 ♭3 ♯4 ♯5 7
1 2 3 ♯5 ♭7	1 ♭3 ♯4 ♯5 ♭7
1 ♯2 3 ♯5 ♭7	1 3 5 ♯6 7
1 2 ♭3 5 ♭6	1 3 ♭5 ♯6 7
1 2 ♭3 ♭5 ♭6	1 3 ♯5 ♯6 7
1 2 ♭3 5 ♭7	1 ♭3 5 ♯6 7
1 2 ♭3 ♭5 ♭7	1 ♭3 ♭5 ♯6 7
1 2 ♭3 ♯5 ♭7	1 ♭3 ♯5 ♯6 7
1 2 ♯2 3 5	1 3 ♯4 5 ♭6
1 2 ♯2 3 ♭5	1 ♭3 ♯4 5 ♭6

5) Six-Note Texture: Hexatonics or Triad Pairs

Hexatonic scales or triad pairs are two triads that don't have any notes in common. Let's look at the hexatonic scales that feature the same kind of triads.

Hexatonics	Intervals
F+/G+ or F+/E♭ + (F whole-tone scale)	1 2 3 ♯4 ♯5 ♭7
E+/F+ = F (augmented scale)	1 ♯2 3 5 ♯5 7
F/E	1 ♯2 3 ♯4 5 7
F-/E-	1 2 ♭3 ♯4 5 7

As you can see, these two triad pairs F+/G+ and F+/E+ become two familiar symmetrical scales:

1) F+/G+=F whole-tone scale: 1 2 3 ♯4 ♯5 ♭7
2) F+/E+=F augmented scale: 1 ♯2 3 5 ♯5 7

6) Seven-Note Texture:

Here are several scale possibilities generated by Mode 1 of double-symmetrical augmented scale:

Scales	Intervals
Lydian ♯6	1 2 3 ♯4 5 ♯6 7
Lydian ♭6	1 2 3 ♯4 5 ♭6 7
Lydian ♭6 ♯2	1 ♯2 3 ♯4 5 ♭6 7
Lydian ♯2 ♯6	1 ♯2 3 ♯4 5 ♯6 7
Lydian ♯2 ♯5 ♯6	1 ♯2 3 ♯4 ♯5 ♯6 7
double harmonic minor	1 2 ♭3 ♯4 5 ♭6 7
Aeolian ♯4	1 2 ♭3 ♯4 5 ♭6 ♭7

7) Eight-Note Texture:

Here are some arpeggio-pair possibilities generated by eight-note textures:

Octatonic	Intervals
FΔ/E♭+7	1 2 3 ♯4 5 ♯5 ♯6 7
F-Δ/E♭+7	1 2 ♭3 ♯4 5 ♯5 ♯6 7
F-Δ/E♭7♭5	1 2 ♯2 3 5 ♯5 ♯6 7
F-Δ♭5/E♭7♭5	1 2 ♯2 3 ♯4 ♯5 ♯6 7
F7/G6(♭5) Resonance Chord	1 2 3 ♯4 5 ♯5 ♭7 7

8) Nine-Note Texture:

It is also possible to combine all nine notes of the double-symmetrical augmented scale:

Nonatonic	Intervals
F+/E+/E♭+	1 2 ♯2 3 ♯4 5 ♯5 ♯6 7
Fo/Ao/C♯o	
F Lyd/A Lyd/C♯ Lyd	
F(♭5)/ G+sus/A♭+sus	
F7/G6 (♭5)add(♯9)	
F augmented+ E augmented scale	
F whole-tone + E augmented scale	

Mode 2

Half-Half-Whole Scale

Dominant Symmetrical Augmented

Mixolydian ♭5 add (♭2, ♭6)

Mode 2 consider of two half steps followed by a whole step in an ascending pattern (hhw). We can also call it the *dominant symmetrical augmented scale.*

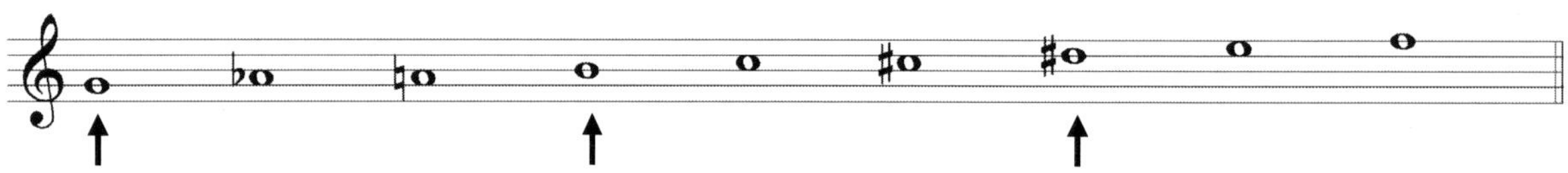

Mode 2: G7♭5(♭9, 9, 11, ♭13, 13) B7♭5(♭9, 9, 11, ♭13, 13) D♯7♭5(♭9, 9, 11, ♭13, 13)

You can see this mode as a Mixolydian ♭5 add (♭2, ♭6).

G A♭ A B C D♭ E♭ E F
1 ♭2 2 3 4 ♭5 ♭6 6 ♭7

The first, fourth and seventh degrees of the scale create a major dominant ♭5 chord with a flatted 9th, a natural 9th, a natural 11th, a flat 13th, and a natural 13th.

Chord:

G7♭5(♭9, 9, 11, ♭13, 13)

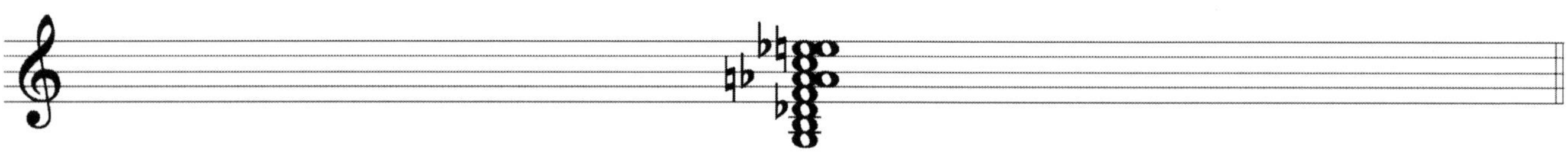

Textures of Mode 2:

1) Two-Note Texture:

♭2, 2, 3, 4, ♯4 or ♭5, ♯5 or ♭6, 6, ♭7.

2) Three-Note Texture:

2.1) Triads

Triads
G+
G(♭5)

2.2) Trichords

1 3 7	1 5 7	1 4 5	Cluster
G7no5	G+7 no 3	G+sus4	1 ♭2 3
	G7♭5 no 3	Gsus4(♭5)	1 ♭2 3
		GLyd(♯5)	1 2 3

3) Four-Note Texture:

3.1) Arpeggios

Arpeggios
G+7
G7♭5

3.2) Melodic Structures

Melodic Structures	
1 2 3 ♭5	1 ♭2 2 ♯5
1 2 3 ♯5	1 ♭2 2 4
1 ♭2 3 ♭5	1 3 4 ♭5
1 ♭2 3 ♯5	1 3 4 ♯5
1 ♭2 2 ♭5	1 3 ♯4 ♯5

4) Five-Note Texture:

Pentatonics	
1 2 3 ♭5 6	1 ♭2 3 ♭5 ♭7
1 2 3 ♯5 6	1 ♭2 3 ♯5 ♭7
1 ♭2 3 ♭5 6	1 ♭2 2 ♭5 ♭7
1 ♭2 3 ♯5 6	1 ♭2 2 ♯5 ♭7
1 ♭2 2 ♭5 6	1 ♭2 2 4 ♭7
1 ♭2 2 ♯5 6	1 3 4 ♭5 ♭6
1 ♭2 2 4 6	1 3 4 ♭5 6

1 2 3 ♭5 ♭6	1 3 4 ♯5 6
1 ♭2 3 ♭5 ♭6	1 3 ♯4 ♯5 6
1 ♭2 2 ♭5 ♭6	1 3 4 ♭5 7
1 ♭2 2 4 ♭6	1 3 4 ♯5 7
1 2 3 ♭5 ♭7	1 3 ♯4 ♯5 7
1 2 3 ♯5 ♭7	

5) Six-Note Texture:

Hexatonics	Intervals
G+/A+, G+/F (G whole-tone scale)	1 2 3 ♯4 ♯5 ♭7
G+/A ♭+, (A♭ augmented scale)	1 ♯2 3 5 ♯5 7

6) Seven-Note Texture:

Scales	Intervals
Mixolydian ♭5	1 2 3 4 ♭5 6 ♭7
Mixolydian ♭5 ♭6	1 2 3 4 ♭5 ♭6 ♭7
Mixolydian ♭5 ♭2	1 ♭2 3 4 ♭5 6 ♭7
Mixolydian ♭5 ♭2 ♭6	1 ♭2 3 4 ♭5 ♭6 ♭7

7) Eight-Note Texture:

Octatonic	Intervals
G7 ♭5/E+Δ	1 ♭2 3 4 ♭5 ♭6 6 ♭7
G+7/E+(6)	1 ♭2 3 4 ♭5 ♭6 6 ♭7

8) Nine-Note Texture:

Nonatonic	Intervals
G+/A♭+/A+	1 ♭2 2 3 4 ♭5 ♭6 6 ♭7
Gsus4(♭5)/Bsus4(♭5)/E♭sus4(♭5)	
G+sus/A ♭+sus/A+Lyd	
G augmented + A♭ augmented scale	
G whole-tone+A♭ augmented scale	

Mode 3

Half-Whole-Half Scale

Tonic Symmetrical Augmented

Tcherepnin Scale

Ionian ♭2 add(♯2, ♭6)/Phrygian major add(♯2,♮6)/Double Harmonic Major (♯2,♮6)

Mode 3 consists of a half step, a whole step and a half step in an ascending pattern (hwh). We can also call it the *tonic symmetrical augmented scale.*

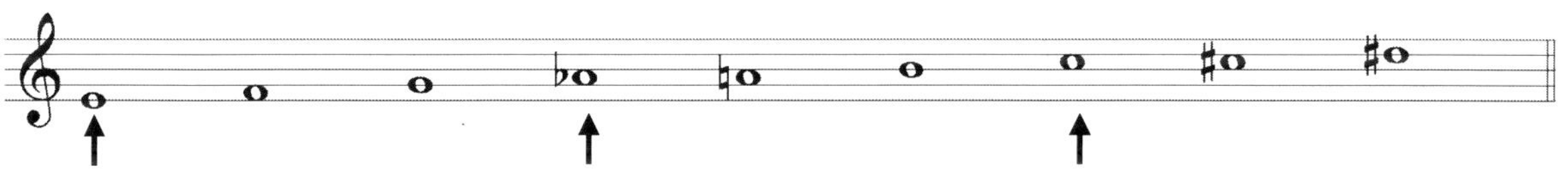

Mode 3: EΔ(♭9,♯9, 11,♭13, 13) AbΔ(♭9,♯9, 11,♭13, 13) CΔ(♭9,♯9, 11,♭13, 13)

You can view this mode as an Ionian ♭2 add (♯2,♭6), Phrygian major add (♯2,♮6) **or** double harmonic major add(♯2,♮6).

E F G G♯ A B C C♯ D♯
1 ♭2 ♯2 3 4 5 ♭6 6 7

The first, fourth and seventh degrees create a major seventh chord with a flat 9th, a sharp 9th, an 11th, a flat 13th, and a natural 13th.

Chord:

EΔ(♭9, ♯9, 11, ♭13, 13)

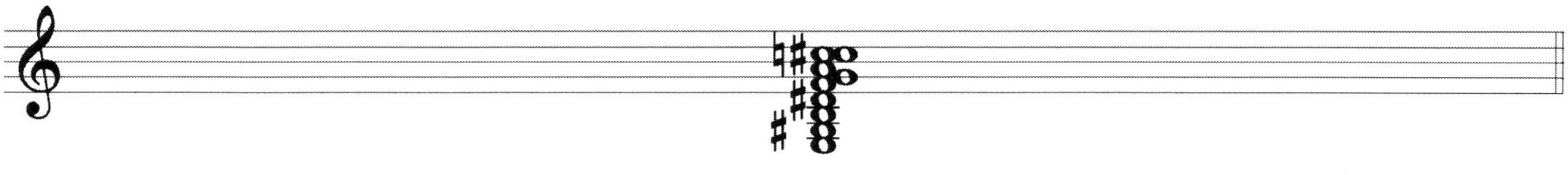

Textures of Mode 3:

1) Two-Note Texture:

♭2, ♯2, 3, 4 , 5, ♭6, 6, 7.

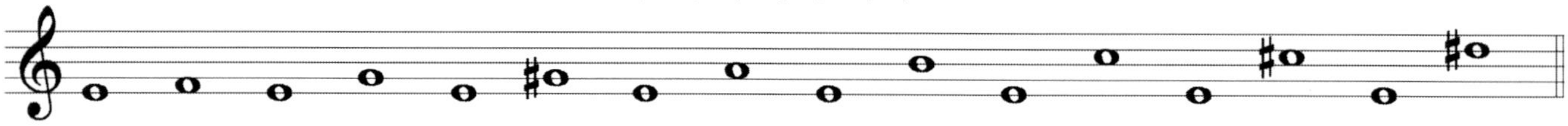

2) Three-Note Texture:

2.1) Triads

Triads
E+
E
E-
Esus4
E Phry (1 ♭2 5)

2.2) Trichords

1 3 7	1 5 7	1 4 5	Cluster
EΔ no 5	E+Δ no3	Esus4	1 ♭2 ♭3
E-Δ no 5	EΔ no3		1 ♭2 3
			1 ♭3 3

3) Four-Note Texture:

3.1) Arpeggios

Arpeggios
E+Δ
EΔ
E-Δ♯5
E-Δ
E+Δsus4
EΔsus4

3.2) Melodic Structures

Melodic Structures	
1 2 3 5	1 ♭2 ♯2 5
1 2 3 ♯5	1 ♭2 ♯2 ♯5
1 ♯2 3 5	1 3 4 5
1 ♯2 3 ♯5	1 3 4 ♯5
1 ♭2 3 5	1 3 5 ♭6
1 ♭2 3 ♯5	1 3 4 ♯5
1 2 ♭3 5	1 ♭3 4 5
1 2 ♭3 ♯5	1 ♭3 4 ♯5
1 ♭2 ♭3 5	1 ♭3 5 ♯6
1 ♭2 ♭3 ♯5	1 ♭3 4 ♯5
1 ♭2 ♯2 3	

4) Five-Note Texture:

Pentatonics	
1 2 3 5 7	1 ♭2 ♭3 5 6
1 2 3 ♯5 7	1 ♭2 ♭3 ♯5 6
1 ♯2 3 5 7	1 ♭2 ♯2 3 6
1 ♯2 3 ♯5 7	1 ♭2 ♯2 5 6
1 ♭2 3 5 7	1 ♭2 ♯2 ♯5 6
1 ♭2 3 ♯5 7	1 3 4 5 7
1 2 ♭3 5 7	1 3 4 ♯5 7
1 2 ♭3 ♯5 7	1 3 5 ♭6 7
1 ♭2 ♭3 5 7	1 3 4 ♯5 7
1 ♭2 ♭3 ♯5 7	1 ♭3 4 57
1 ♭2 ♯2 3 7	1 ♭3 4 ♯5 7
1 ♭2 ♯2 5 7	1 ♭3 5 ♭6 7
1 ♭2 ♯2 ♯5 7	1 ♭3 4 ♯5 7
1 2 3 5 6	1 3 4 5 6
1 2 3 ♯5 6	1 3 4 ♯5 6
1 ♯2 3 5 6	1 3 5 ♭6 6
1 ♯2 3 ♯5 6	1 3 4 ♯5 6
1 ♭2 3 5 6	1 ♭3 4 5 6
1 ♭2 3 ♯5 6	1 ♭3 4 ♯5 6
1 2 ♭3 5 6	1 ♭3 5 ♭6 6
1 2 ♭3 ♯5 6	1 ♭3 4 ♯5 6

5) Six-Note Texture:

Hexatonics	Intervals
E+/E♭+=E augmented scale	1 2 3 ♯4 ♯5 ♭7
E+/F+ = F augmented scale	1 ♯2 3 5 ♯5 7
E/F	1 ♭2 3 4 5 ♭6
E-/F-	1 ♭2 ♯2 3 5 ♭6

6) Seven-Note Texture:

Scales	Intervals
Ionian ♯2	1 ♯2 3 4 5 6 7
Ionian ♭2	1 ♭2 3 4 5 6 7
Ionian ♭2 ♭6=double harmonic major	1 ♭2 3 4 5 ♭6 7
Ionian ♯2 ♭6	1 ♯2 3 4 5 ♭6 7
Ionian ♯5 ♯2	1 ♯2 3 4 ♯5 6 7
Ionian ♯5 ♭2	1 ♭2 3 4 ♯5 6 7
Phrygian natural 7=harmonic minor ♭2	1 ♭2 ♭3 4 5 ♭6 7
melodic minor ♭2	1 ♭2 ♭3 4 5 6 7
melodic minor ♯5 ♭2	1 ♭2 ♭3 4 ♯5 6 7

7) Eight-Note Texture:

Octatonic	Intervals
EΔ/D♭+Δ	1 ♭2 3 4 5 ♭6 6 7
E-Δ/D♭+Δ	1 ♭2 ♭3 4 5 ♭6 6 7
E+Δ/D♭+7	1 ♭2 3 4 5 ♭6 6 7
E-Δ♯5/D♭+7	1 ♭2 ♭3 4 5 ♭6 6 7

8) Nine-Note Texture:

Nonatonic	Intervals
E+/F+/G+	1 2 ♯2 3 ♯4 5 ♯5 ♯6 7
Esus4/A♭sus4/Csus4	
A♭+sus/F+Lyd/G+sus	
E augmented scale+ F augmented scale	
E augmented scale + F whole-tone scale	

Notation of the Modes and Chords of the Double-Symmetrical Augmented Scale

For the sake of simplicity, I recommend the following notation.

Scale/mode examples:

Scale/Mode	Example in the key of C
Mode 1	C whh
Mode 2	C hhw
Mode 3	C hwh

Chord examples:

Scale/Mode	Chord examples in the key of C
Mode 1	CΔ whh C-Δ(♯5) whh C+Δ(♯9,♯13) whh Csus2 whh C-7 whh etc.
Mode 2	C+hhw C+7(♭9) hhw C7sus4(♭5) hhw C+7(♭9,13) hhw etc.
Mode 3	C-Δ♯5 hwh C+Δsus4 hwh CΔsus4(♭9) hwh C-Δ♯5 hwh etc.

III. Chords & Voicings

The double-symmetrical augmented scale produces a unique and harmonically rich sound. Below are a few examples of chord voicings that might inspire you to create your own lines and chord progressions.

Mode 1 Voicings

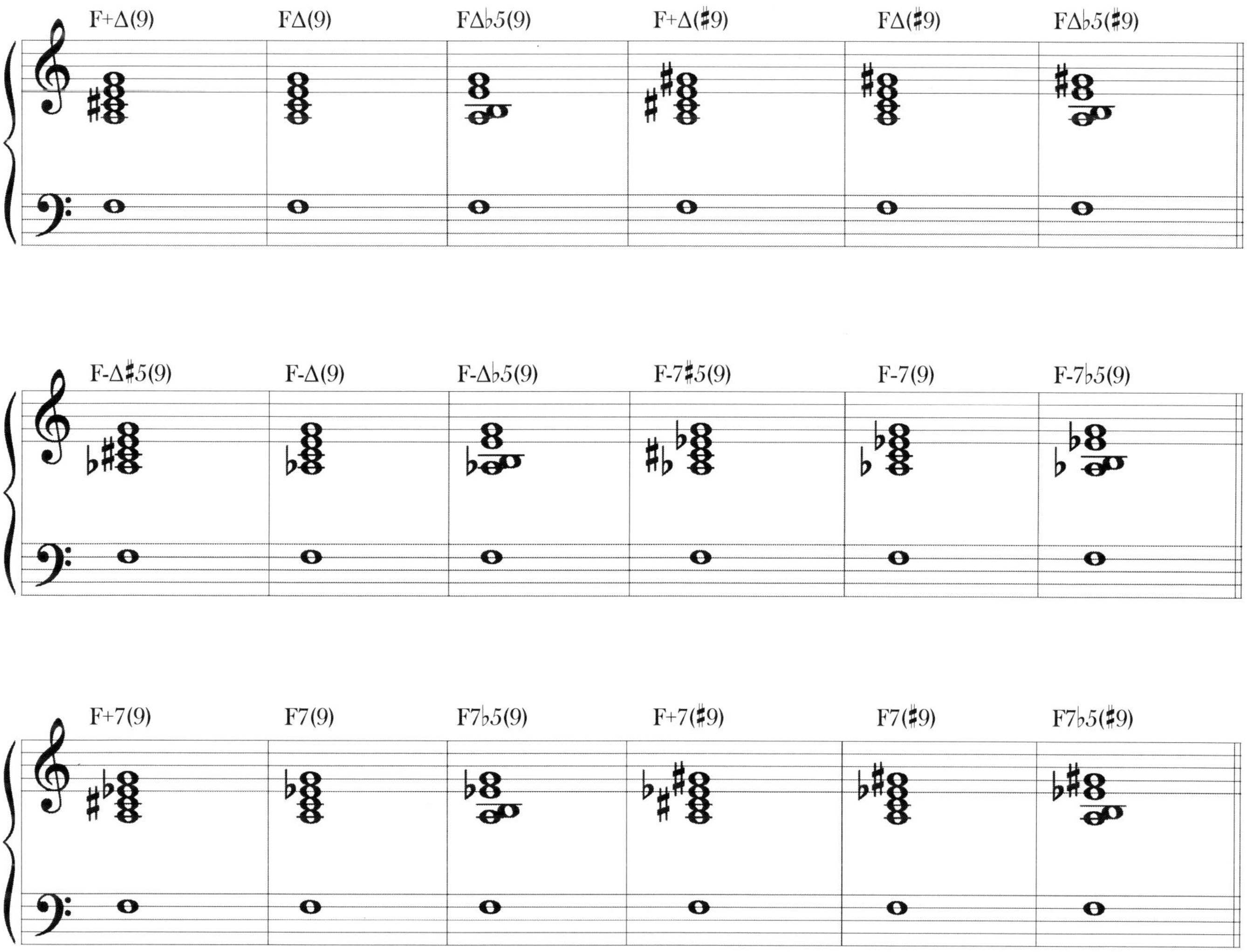

Mode 2 Voicings

13

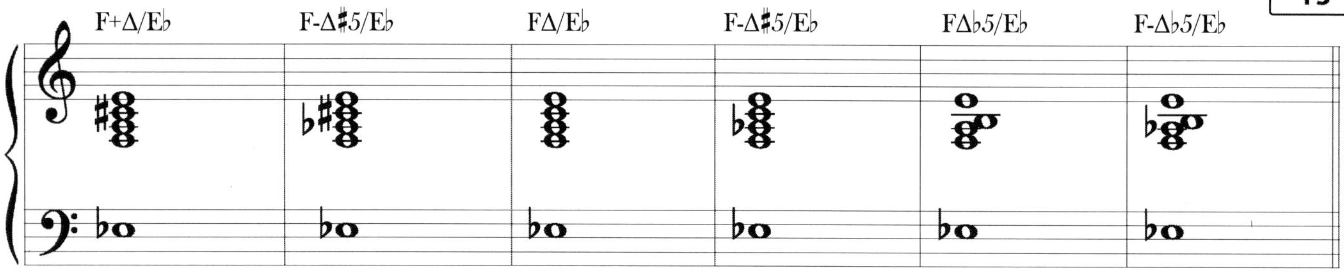

More options:

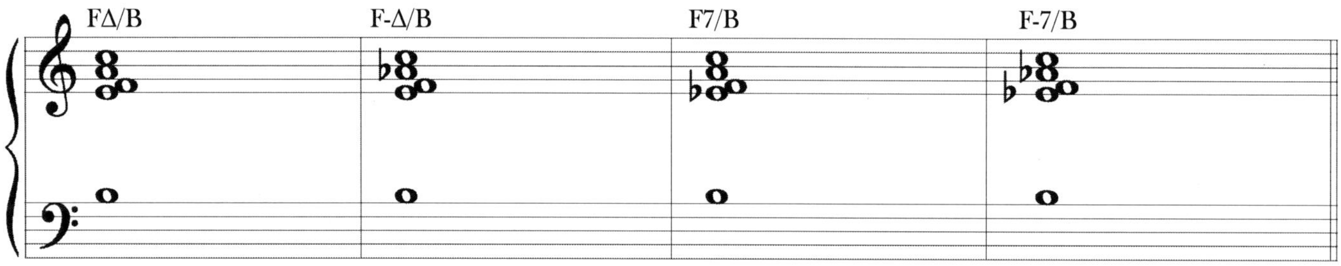

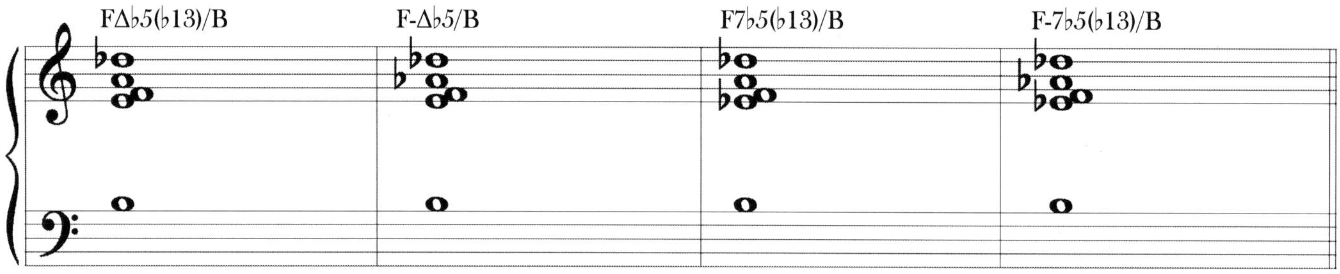

Mode 3 Voicings

14

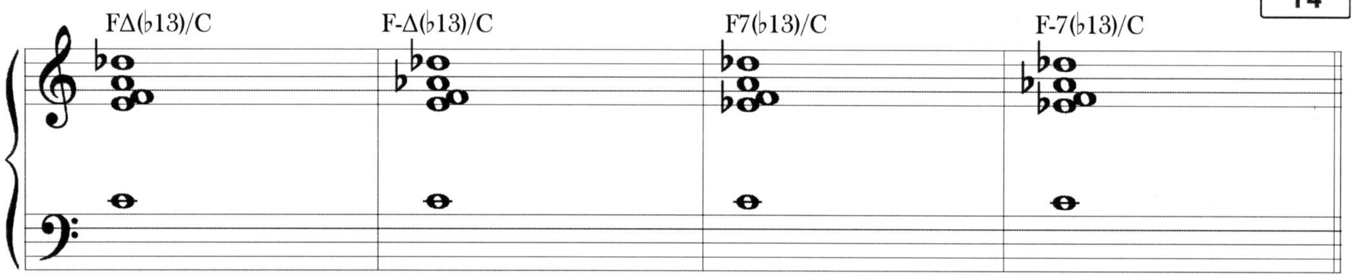

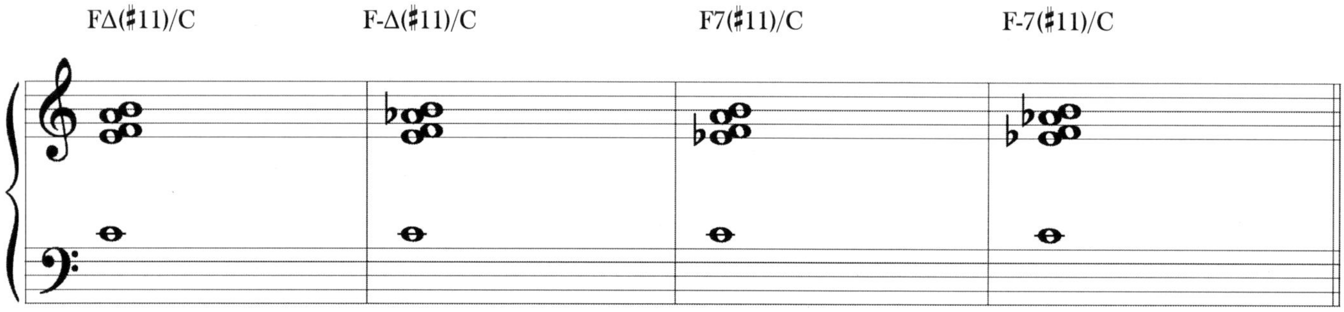

Here are some interesting orchestrations used by Hubert Nuss, a prominent German pianist specializing in Messiaen's music:

Next, some additional possibilities:

Mode 1 Inversions:

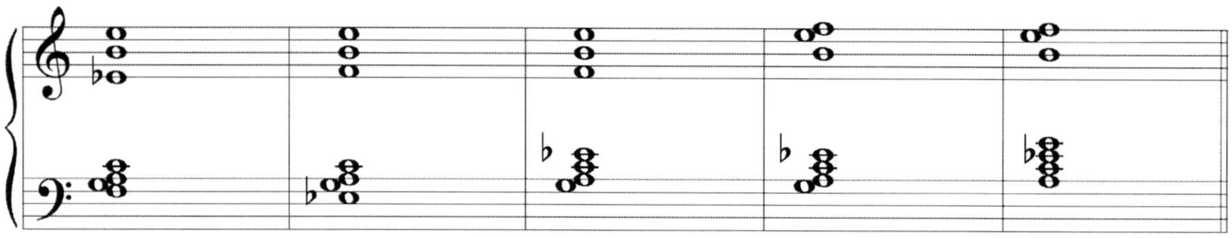

Mode 2 Voicing Orchestrations:

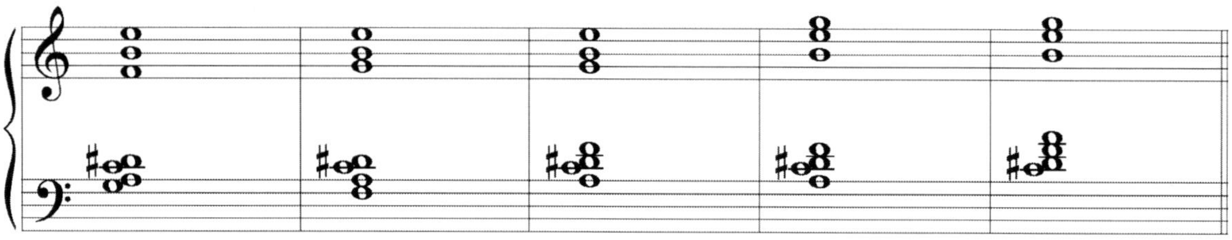

Mode 3 Cluster:

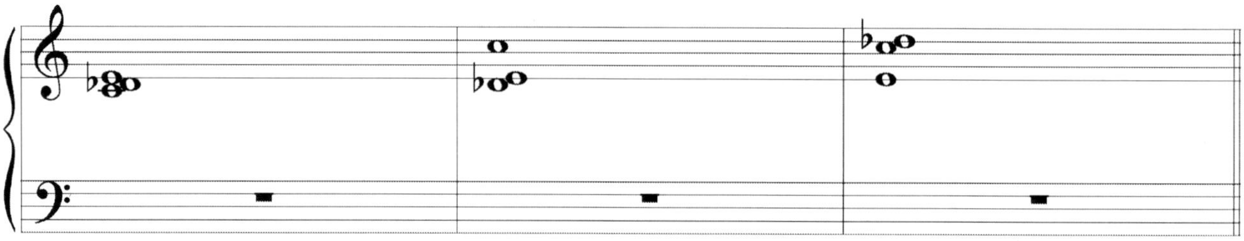

Mode 3 Pentatonic Voicings:

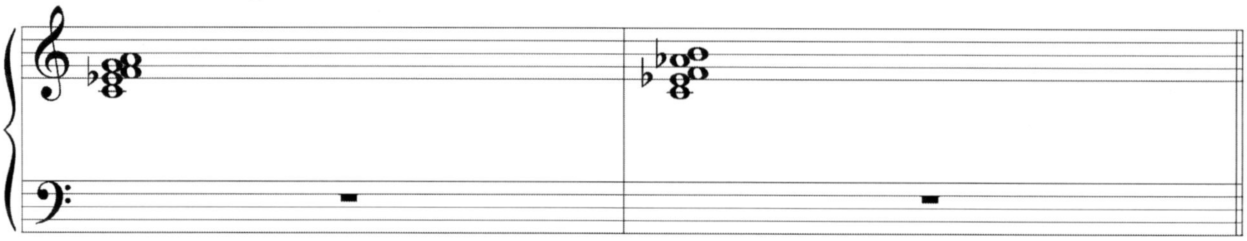

Eight-Note Voicings:

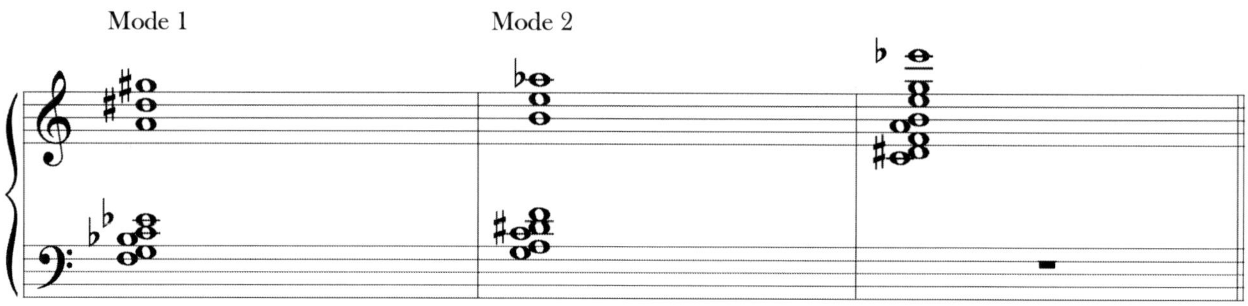

Hybrid Chords

Hybrid chords are chords that do not have a third. Like inversions, they are represented with a slash. Unlike inversions, their bass note does not belong to the chord triad. Chords with a seventh as their bass note can be considered hybrid however.

Here's a list of hybrid chords based on different chord options of Mode 1:

	2	♯2/♭3	3	♯4/♭5	5	♯5	♯6	7
F+Δ	F+Δ/G	F+Δ/A♭	-	F+Δ/B	F+Δ/C	-	F+Δ/E♭	F+Δ/E
FΔ	FΔ/G	FΔ/A♭	-	FΔ/B	-	FΔ/C♯	FΔ/E♭	FΔ/E
FΔ♭5	FΔ♭5/G	FΔ♭5/A♭	-	-	FΔ♭5/C	FΔ♭5/C♯	FΔ ♭5/E♭	FΔ♭5/E
F-Δ♯5	F-Δ♯5/G	-	F-Δ♯5/A	F-Δ♯5/B	F-Δ♯5/C	-	F-Δ♯5/E♭	F-Δ♯5/E
F-Δ	F-Δ/G	-	F-Δ/A	F-Δ/B	-	F-Δ/C♯	F-Δ/E♭	F-Δ/E
F-Δ♭5	F-Δ♭5/G	-	F-Δ♭5/A	-	F-Δ♭5/C	F-Δ♭5/C♯	F-Δ♭5/E♭	F-Δ♭5/E
F+7	F+7/G	F+7/A♭	-	F+7/B	F+7/C	-	F+7/E♭	F+7/E
F7	F7/G	F7/A♭	-	F7/B	-	F7/C♯	F7/E♭	F7/E
F7♭5	F7♭5/G	F7♭5/A♭	-	-	F7♭5/C	F7♭5/C♯	F7♭5/E♭	F7♭5/E
F-Δ♯5	F-Δ♯5/G	-	F-Δ♯5/A	F-Δ♯5/B	F-Δ♯5/C	-	F-Δ♯5/E♭	F-Δ♯5/E
F-7	F-7/G	-	F-7/A	F-7/B	-	F-7/C♯	F-7/E♭	F-7/E
F-7♭5	F-7♭5/G	-	F-7♭5/A	-	F-7♭5/C	F-7♭5/C♯	F-7♭5/E♭	F-7♭5/E

Hybrid chords based on different chord options of Mode 2:

	♭2	2	3	4	♯11/♭5	♯5/♭6	6	♭7
G+7	G+7/A♭	G+7/A	-	G+7/C	G+7/C♯	-	G+7/E	G+7/F
G7♭5	G7♭5/A♭	G7♭5/A	-	G7♭5/C	-	G7♭5/E♭	G7♭5/E	G7♭5/F

Hybrid chords based on different chord options of Mode 3:

	♭2	♯2/ ♭3	3	4	5	♯5/♭6	6	7
E+Δ	E+Δ/F	E+Δ/G	-	E+Δ/A	E+Δ/B	-	E+Δ/C♯	E+Δ/D♯
EΔ	EΔ/F	EΔ/G	-	EΔ/A	-	EΔ/C	EΔ/C♯	EΔ/D♯
E-Δ♯5	E-Δ♯5/F	-	E-Δ♯5/A♭	E-Δ♯5/A	E-Δ♯5/B	-	E-Δ♯5/C♯	E-Δ♯5/D♯
E-Δ	E-Δ/F	-	E-Δ/A♭	E-Δ/A	-	E-Δ/C	E-Δ/C♯	E-Δ♯5/D♯
E+Δsus4	E+Δsus4/F	E+Δsus4/G	E+Δsus4/A♭	-	E+Δsus4/B	-	E+Δsus4/C♯	E+Δsus4/D♯
EΔsus4	EΔsus4/F	EΔsus4/G	EΔsus4/A♭	-	-	EΔsus4/C	EΔsus4/C♯	EΔsus4/D♯

Polychords & Tonal Expansions

Triads and seventh chords layered on top of another triad or seventh chord are called *polychords.* They are usually represented with a horizontal line separating one triad or seventh chord from the other. These superstructures can be made up of either tensions or chord tones plus tensions.

Here are some examples of polychords comprising two chords of the same kind, built from the first, second and third modes of the scale:

Mode 1:

Mode 1 Polychords
E+Δ / F+Δ
EΔ / FΔ
E-Δ / F- Δ
E-Δ♯5 / F-Δ♯5

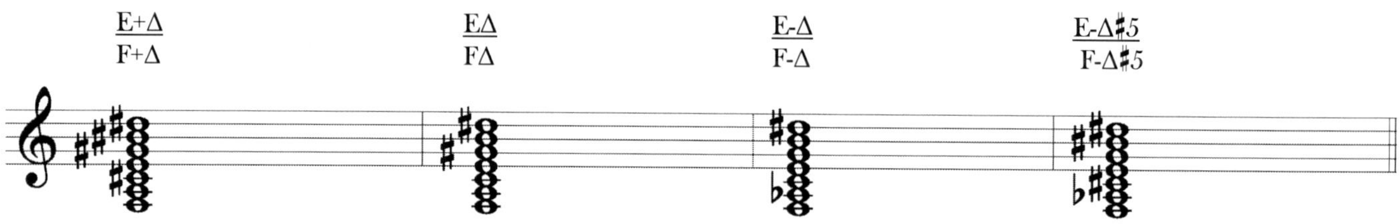

Mode 2:

Mode 2 Polychords
F+7 / G+7
F7♭5 / G7♭5

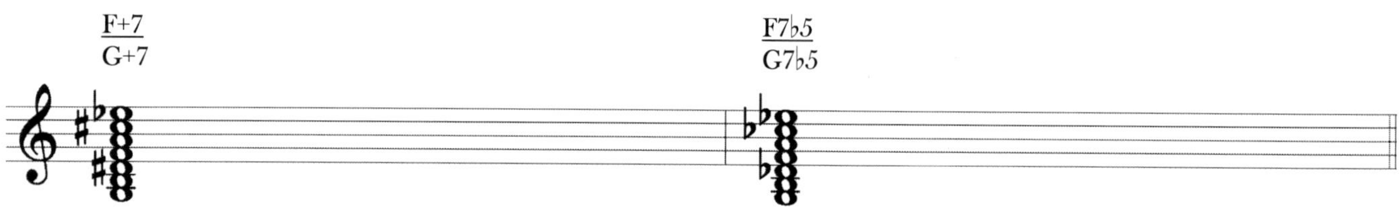

Mode 3:

Mode 3 Polychords
B+ / C+
B+sus4 / C+sus4

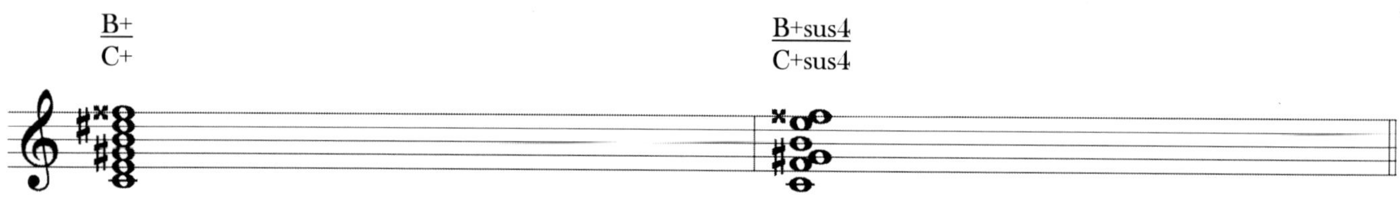

When played melodically, polychords become *tonal expansions.*

IV. Rules for Using the Double-Symmetrical Augmented Scale

Access Points

Access points are notes within each chord from which we can access specific modes of the double-symmetrical augmented scale. They are usually in the upper-structure triads of the chord.

Substitutions

Here are the most common harmonic substitutions:

Tonic Major

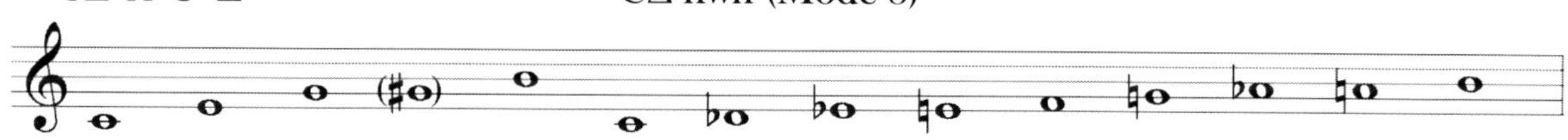

Tonic Δ or Δ(♯5)	Mode
1	3
3	3
5	2
♯5	3
7	2

Tonic Minor

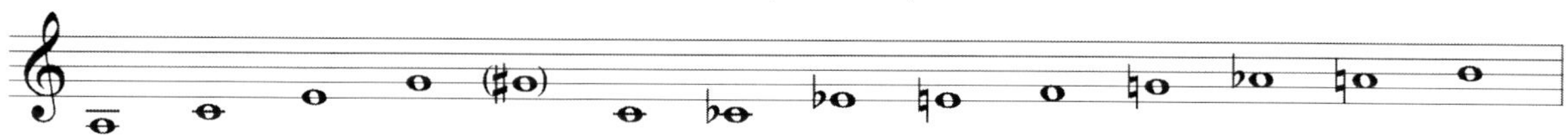

Tonic -7 or -Δ	Mode
1	1
♭3	3
5	3
♭7	2
7	3

Non-Tonic Minor

D-7 or D-Δ FΔ whh (Mode 1)

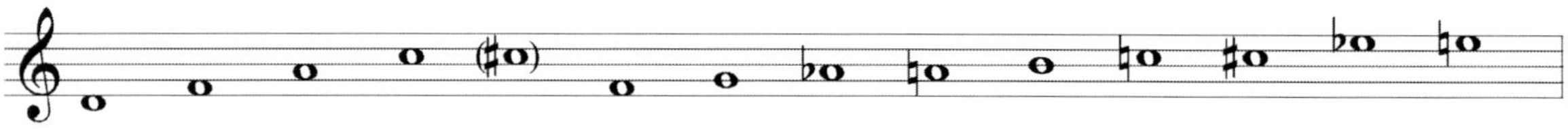

A.P 1 ♭3 5 ♭7 7 ♭3 5 ♭7 7

-7 or -Δ	Mode
1	NCT*
♭3	1
5	1
♭7	3
7	1

*Non-Chord Tone

Subdominant Minor

B-7♭5 B7♭5 hhw (Mode 2)

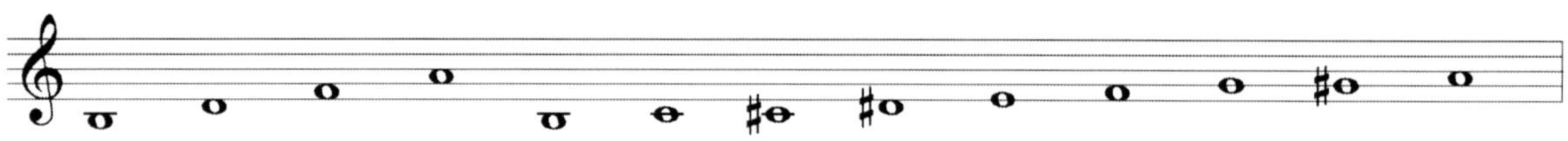

A.P 1 ♭5 ♭7 1 ♭5 ♭7

-7♭5	Modes
1	3
♭3	NCT*
♭5	3
♭7	2

*Non-Chord Tone

Non-Tonic Major or Major ♯5

FΔ or F+Δ FΔ whh (Mode 1)

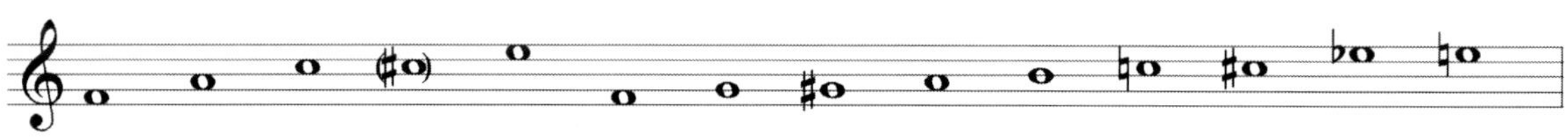

A.P 1 3 5 ♯5 7 1 3 5 ♯5 7

Δ or Δ(♯5)	Mode
1	1
3	1
5	3
♯5	1
7	3

Dominants

G7 or G7♯11 G7♭5 hhw (Mode 2)

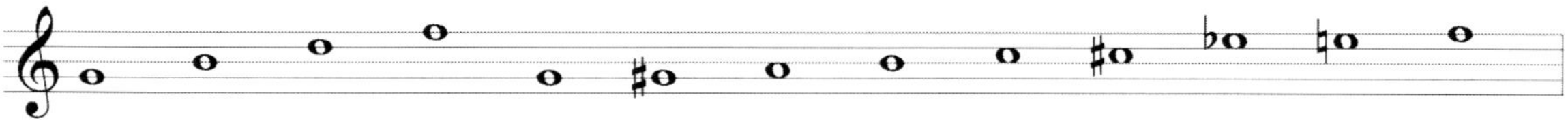

A.P 1 3 5 ♭7 1 3 ♭7

E7♭9 ♭13 or E7♭9 E∆ hwh (Mode 3)

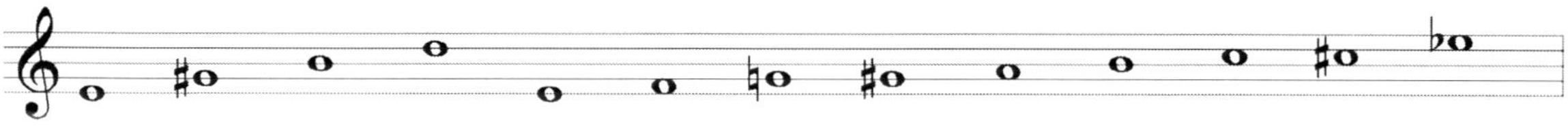

A.P 1 3 5 ♭7 1 3 5

D♭7alt or D♭7alt(♮5) F∆ whh (Mode 1)

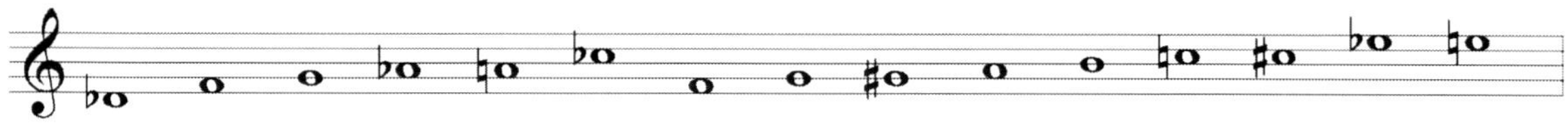

A.P 1 3 ♭5 5 ♯5 ♭7 3 ♭5 5 ♯5 ♭7 1

A7♭13 A∆ whh (Mode 1)

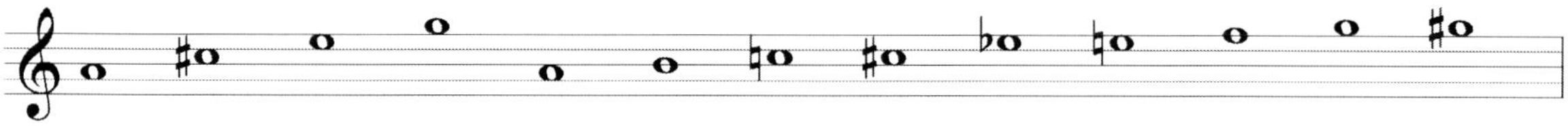

A.P 1 3 5 ♭7 1 3 5 ♭7

	7sus4, 7♯11	7♭9♭13, 7 ♭9	7alt, 7alt(♮5)	7♭13
1	2	3	1	1
3	2	3	1	1
♭5/♯11	1	NCT*	2	NCT*
5	NCT*	2	3	3
♯5/ ♭13	NCT*	3	1	1
♭7	1	NCT*	2	2

*Non-Chord Tone

Diminished

F°7 F∆ whh (Mode 1)

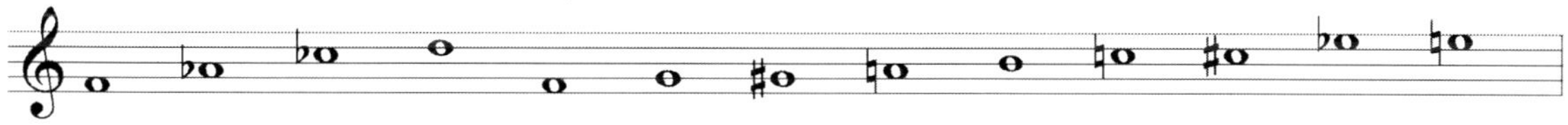

A.P 1 ♭3 ♭5 ♭♭7 1 ♭3 ♭5 7

°∆	Mode
1	1
♭3	3
♭5	2
6(♭♭7)	NCT*
7	3

*Non-Chord Tone

V. Voice Leading

Voice leading entails smoothly connecting the notes from one chord to the next by keeping note movements as close to chromatic as possible and avoiding movements bigger than a major third. This is essential for melodic consistency during improvisation. You must pay attention to both external and internal voice leading.

External Voice Leading

External voice leading occurs between two specific chords. For our purposes, this will be connecting the chord-scale and the double-symmetrical augmented scale.

Internal Voice Leading

Internal voice leading is derived from the scale possibilities arising from the double-symmetrical augmented scale. The table below shows some possible **landing chord tones**, the mode that can be activated as a result from playing a particular tone, and how far the new root note is from the former (interval). Some of the modes that could be activated when the landing chord tone has a function different from 1 are also displayed.

Here's an example:

We suppose that we land in (play) G♯ chord tone of the double-symmetrical augmented scale. Assuming that we're in G♯ hwh (mode 3). If we look at the table on the right (mode 3), we can conclude that G♯ could function either as a ♭3, a 5 or a 7 of mode 1 (whh); or as a 3 or a ♯5/♭6 of the same mode we're in. Therefore, it is crucial to keep voice leading in mind while using this kind of scale to avoid catastrophic results!

Δ whh (Mode 1)		
Chord Tone	Mode	Interval
1	=	-
3	=	♭6
♭5	2	♯4
♭6/♯5	=	3
♭7	2	2

7♭5 hhw (Mode 2)		
Chord Tone	Mode	Interval
1	=	-
♭3	3	6
3	=	♭6
♯4	1	♭5
5	3	4
♯5	=	3
♭7	1	2
7	3	♭2

Δ hwh (Mode3)		
Chord Tone	Mode	Interval
1	=	-
♭3	1	6
3	=	♭6
5	1	4
♯5/♭6	=	3
7	1	2

One excellent musician who masterfully put this concept into practice is sax player Mark Turner. Here are some examples:

1) The ♯9 of the previous chord becomes the maj7 of the new chord, a major 3rd higher.

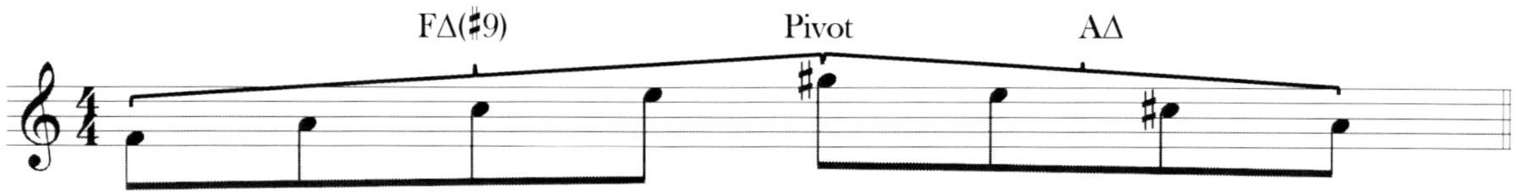

2) The maj7 of the previous chord becomes the ♭3 of the new chord, a major 3rd lower.

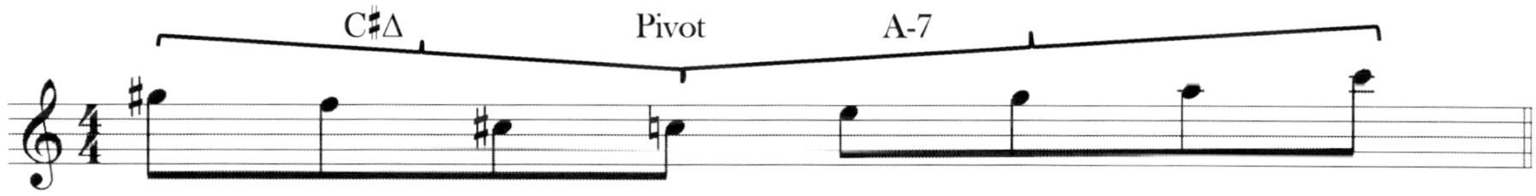

3) The tonic of the new chord is a half step above the ♭3 of the previous chord, a major 3rd higher.

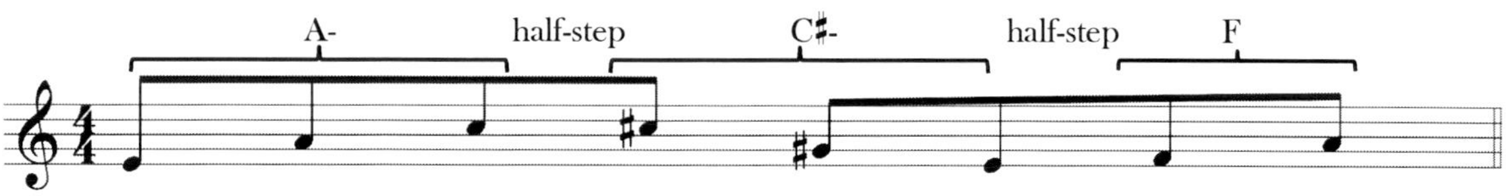

4) Major/minor 3rd combinations.

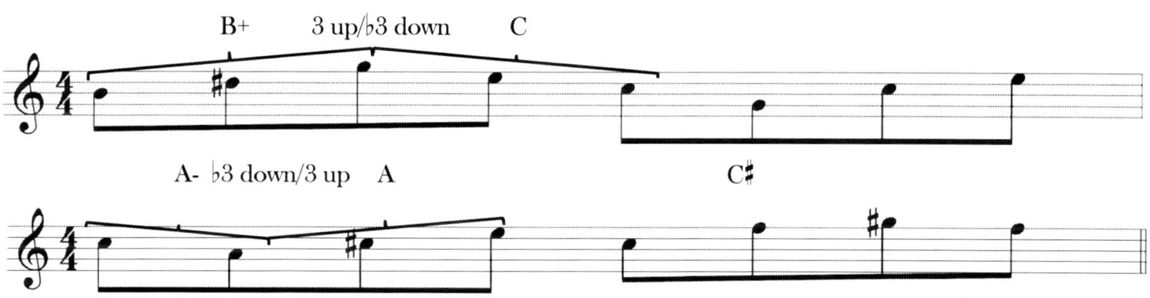

5) Pivot note: the 5th of the previous chord becomes the maj7 of the new chord, a major 3rd lower.

6) The ♭7th of the previous chord becomes the 9th of the new chord, a flat 6th higher.

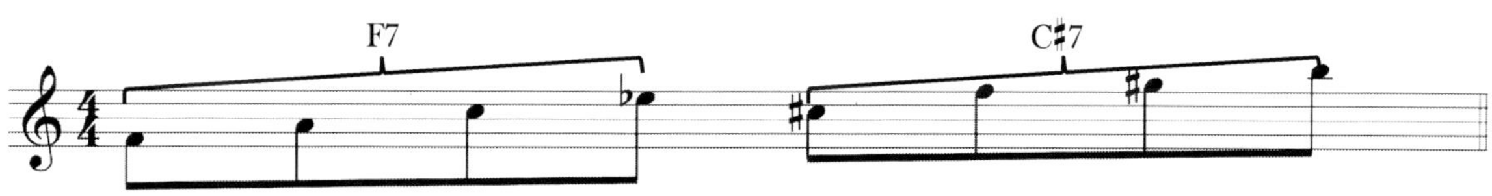

VI. Musical Examples & Exercises

This section illustrates different uses and exercises of the double-symmetrical augmented scale.

Scale Motives and Patterns Examples

Motives

Allan Holdsworth often played the scale using leaps.

Nelson Veras tried to emulate human speech patterns.

Mark Turner played this 2 7 1 3 motif which can also be used as a pattern.

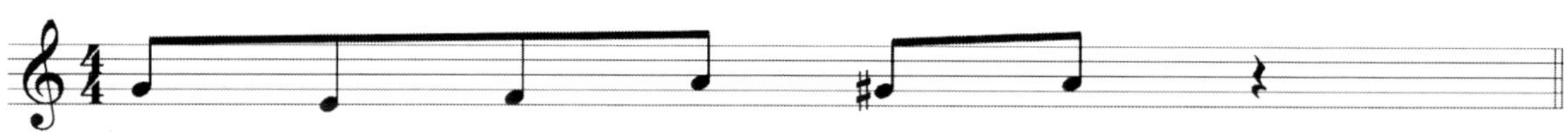

Here's other motif by Mark Turner, this time based on Mode 2.

Uses of Scales Implicit Within the Double-Symmetrical Augmented Scale

Allan Holdsworth emphasized the E hexatonic augmented scale.

One of Mark Turner's Mixolydian ideas: a 4 3 1 ♭7 descending pattern from Mode 3.

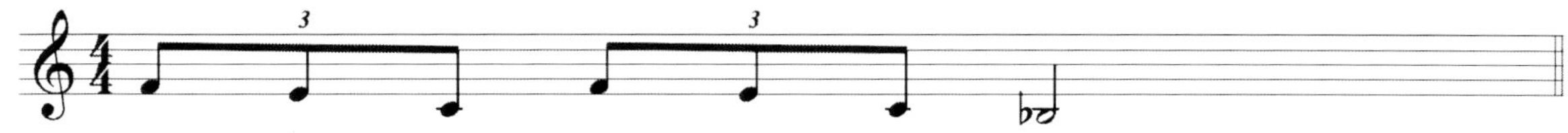

Nelson Veras played a B double-harmonic major followed by a G♭ major triad.

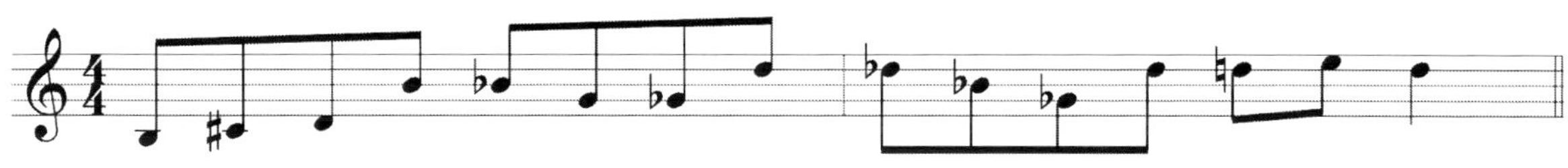

Patterns

Allan Holdsworth played intervals of thirds followed by a classic bebop 1 7 ♭7 1 pattern.

Jerry Bergonzi played a different pattern of the F double-symmetrical augmented scale in different modes:

1) Five descending notes followed by four ascending notes, landing on a note from Mode 1 (a major 3rd lower).

2) A descending pattern in Mode 3.

3) A 1 2 ♭3 7 pattern repeated in ascending major 3rds.

4) A ♭3 2 1 5 pattern (Mode 1) repeated in descending major 3rds.

Nelson Veras combined varius modes and pattern ideas:

1) An ascending pattern based on major triads:

2) A 4 ♭3 1 descending pattern in Mode 3.

3) A pattern based on Mode 1.

4) Lastly, a pattern based on Mode 2.

Scale-Pattern Exercises

Here are some II-7 V7alt IΔ examples. We'll be using a B double-symmetrical augmented scale over a G7 altered chord.

Ascending

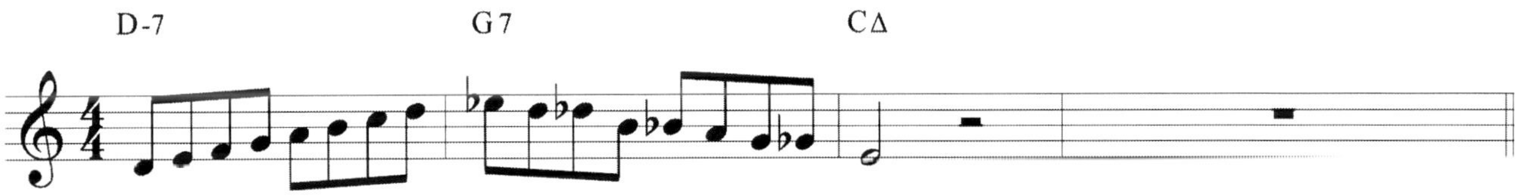

Descending

Ascending (short)

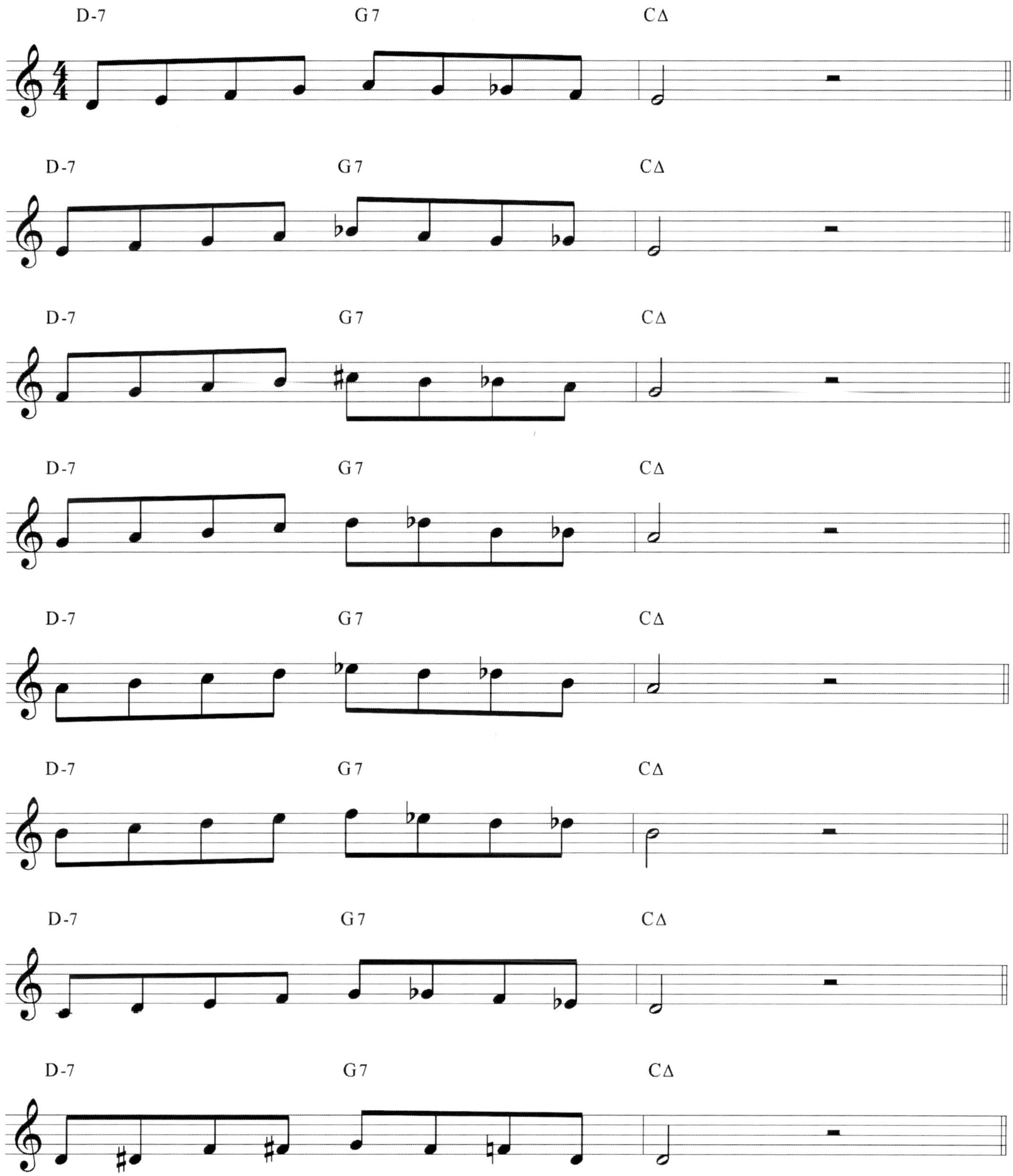

Descending (short)

Suggested next steps....

1. Develop lines in minor (II-7♭5 V7alt I-)
2. Develop lines on other types of dominants
3. Practice in all keys
4. Include other textures
5. Play in context (Whenever possible, you should play these scales in context, that is— use them in a real song or jazz standard.)

Intervallic Examples

An ascending Mode 1 pattern in major 3rds.

An ascending and descending pattern in major 3rds.

Allan Holdsworth's descending patterns in major 3rds.

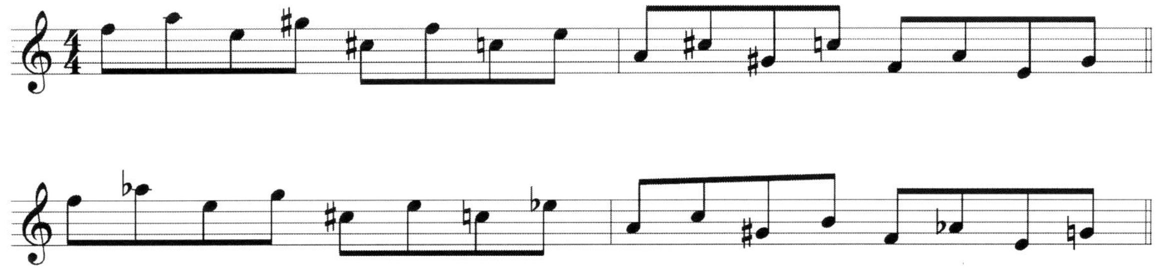

A diatonic pattern in 5ths.

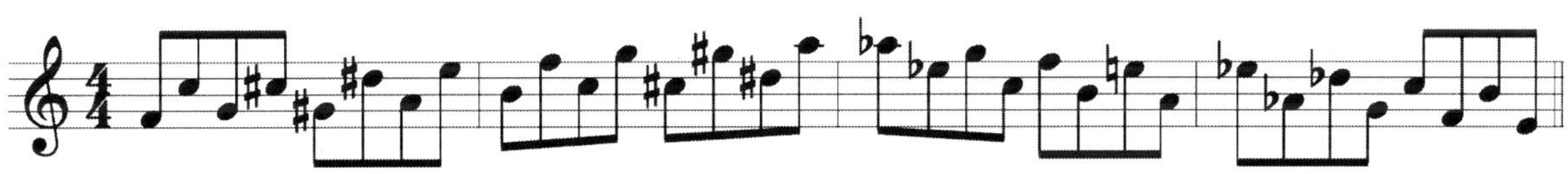

A diatonic pattern in ascending 5ths and descending major 3rds.

Guitarist Nelson Veras played this harmonic idea emphasizing ♯4 and 5 intervals.

Intervallic Exercises

Here are a few patterns of 3rds that use modes 1 and 3 of the double-symmetrical augmented scale:

We can also combine all of the modes:

Suggested next steps....

1. Develop patterns with all kinds of intervals
2. Play in all four double-symmetrical augmented scales
3. Use scale fragments between interval patterns (à la Holdsworth)

Example:

Application

Here's an example of intervallic textures in a IΔ V7alt progression.

16

Now, try using the same concept on the following chord progression. The track goes on for about 4 minutes, giving you a plenty of time to get your feet wet.

17

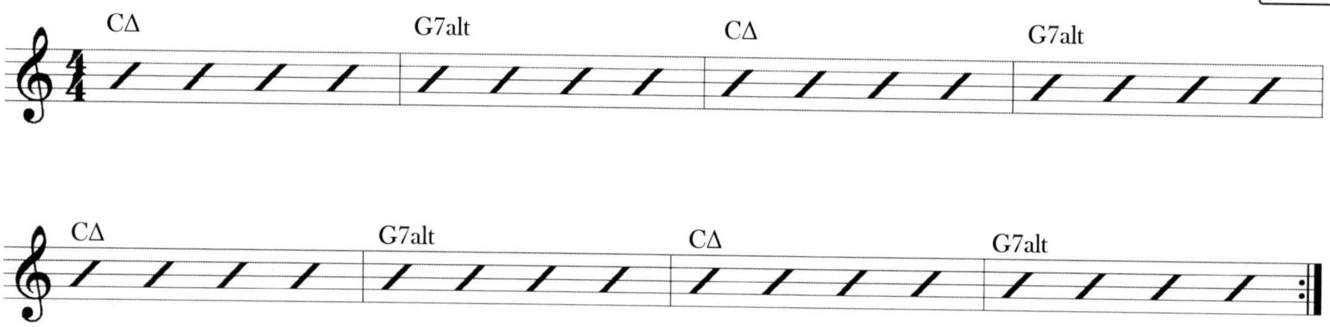

Three-Note Texture Examples

Mark Turner used this three-note cluster idea: 1 2 ♭2.

An example of major triads descending in major 3rds.

A flat-6th ascending pattern by Edward Tomassi, featuring a melodic minor fragment (5 ♭3 2 1) followed by an augmented triad starting from 7th degree of the melodic minor scale.

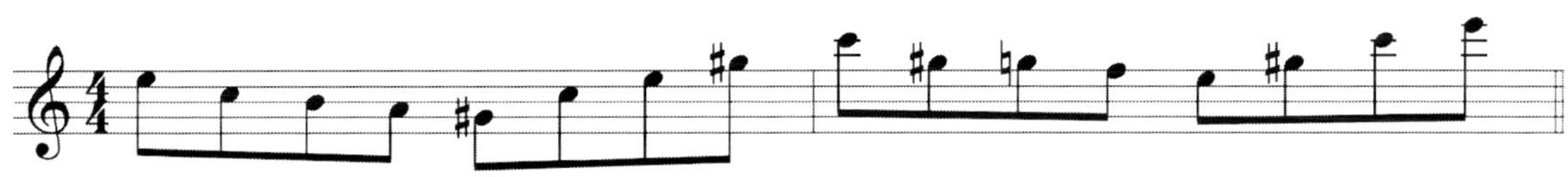

A pattern based on augmented triads in ascending 4ths.

Gary Thomas played sus2 patterns in major 3rds in these two ways:

1)

2)

Tim Miller used different three-note patterns:

1) The first phrase is based on a 1 2 ♭5 over Modes 1 and 2.

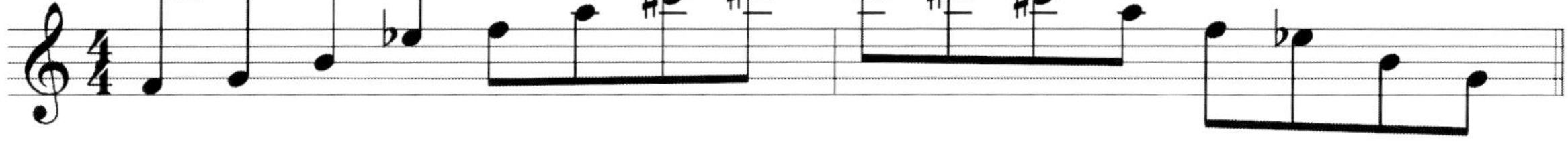

2) 1 2 ♯5 over Modes 1 and 3.

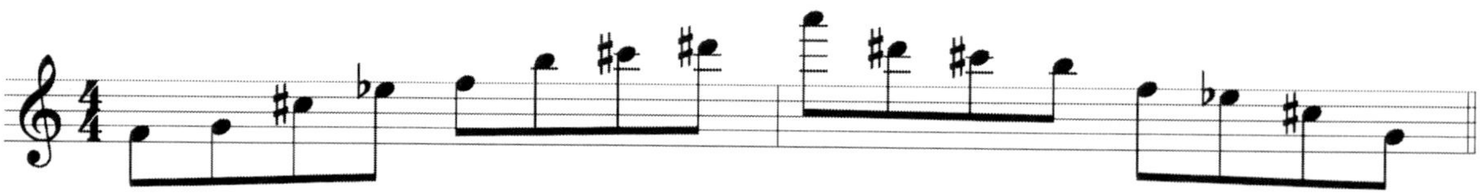

3) 1 3 ♯5 over Modes 1 and 3.

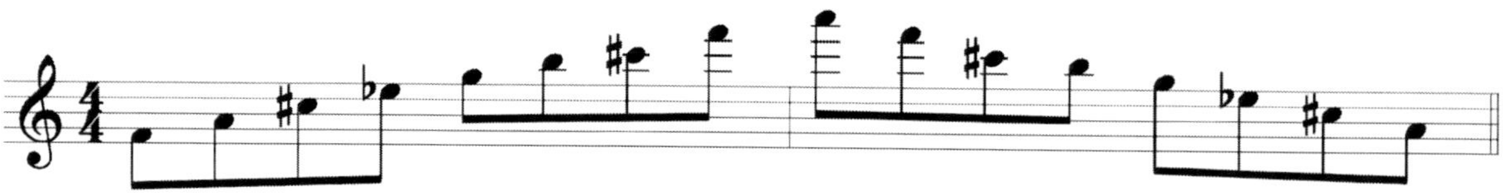

A sus4 triad example.

Jonathan Kreisberg used a 7sus4 (no 5) texture in major 3rds based on Mode 2.

An example featuring the Lydian triad.

Another example with the sus4(♭5) triad.

An example based on an idea by Kurt Rosenwinkel and Mark Turner: F-, C♯- and A- ascending triads, and A♭ -, C-7 and E- descending triads.

Allan Holdsworth played a 1 3 7 and 5 ♭2 1 3 in descending major thirds.

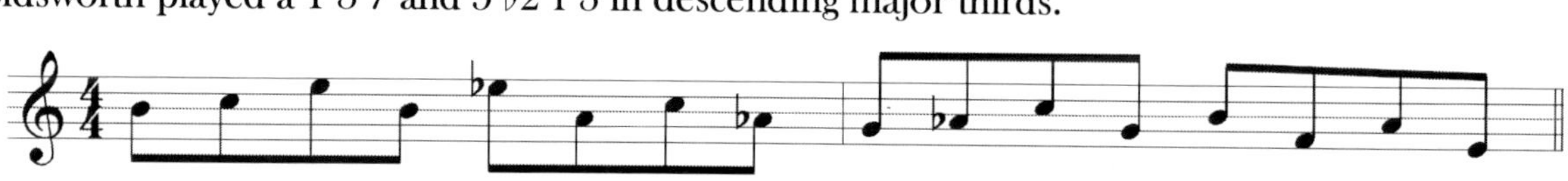

Here is a 1 3 7 texture with rhythm displacement.

Three-Note Texture Exercises

1) Triadic Exercises:

Suggested next steps....

1. Develop patterns in all kinds of three-note texture (all modes)
2. Play the patterns in all four double-symmetrical augmented scales (twelve keys)
3. Play in context

2) Never-Ending Patterns (Triads or Arpeggios)

If you want to internalize the sound of the scale, never-ending patterns provide a good starting point. These patterns combine an ascending three- or four-note texture (in a single mode) with a scale which descends until it finds a note belonging to the same mode, a 3rd up or a 3rd down (♭6 up). Then, the pattern begins again.

Here's a 1-5 triad of F, A or C♯ whh (double-symmetrical augmented scale or Mode 1):

Up a major 3rd

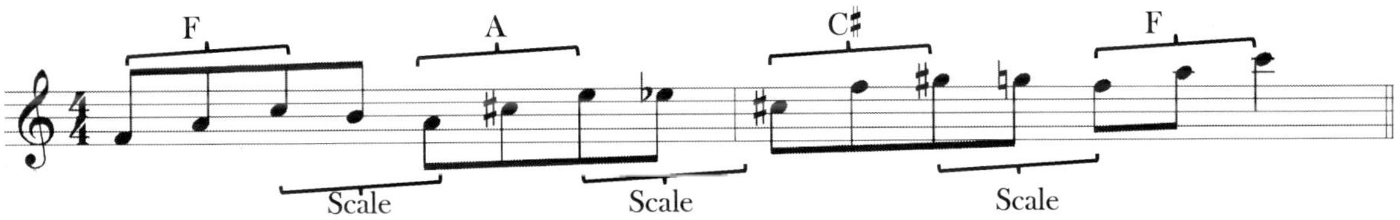

Down a major 3rd

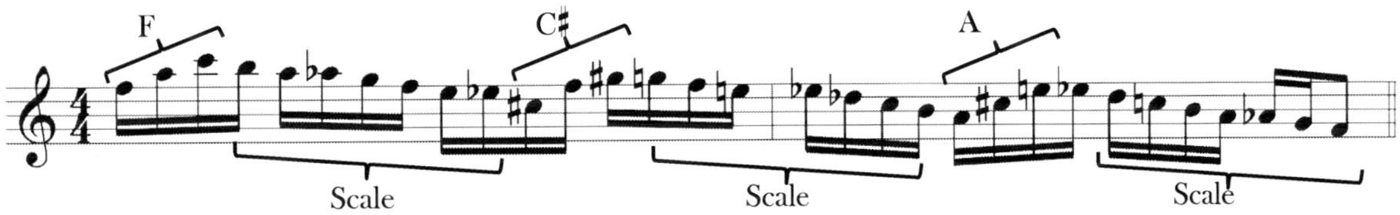

Next, G, B or E♭ hhw (Mode 2):

Up a major 3rd

Down major 3rd

E, A♭, C hwh (Mode 3):

Up a major 3rd

Down a major 3rd

Using a 1-7 arpeggio in Mode 1:

Up a major 3rd

Using a four-part 1-1 arpeggio in Mode 1:

Up a major 3rd

Up a minor 6th

Suggested next steps....

Play this pattern using different arpeggios or triad possibilities

First, choose a mode:

whh (Mode 1)	hhw (Mode 2)	hwh (Mode 3)
+Δ	+7	+Δ
Δ	7♭5	Δ
Δ♭5		-Δ♯5
-Δ♯5		-Δ
-Δ		+Δsus4
-Δ♭5		Δsus4
+7		
7		
7♭5		
-7♯5		
-7		
-7♭5		
*Any combination of Sus2		

Next, create your pattern over your targeted chord types. You may have chosen:

1. One chord type
2. Two chord types
3. Three chord types

Below is an example of a 1-7 Mode 3 in ascending 3rds over three different chords (E+Δ, A♭-Δ♯5, C+Δsus4).

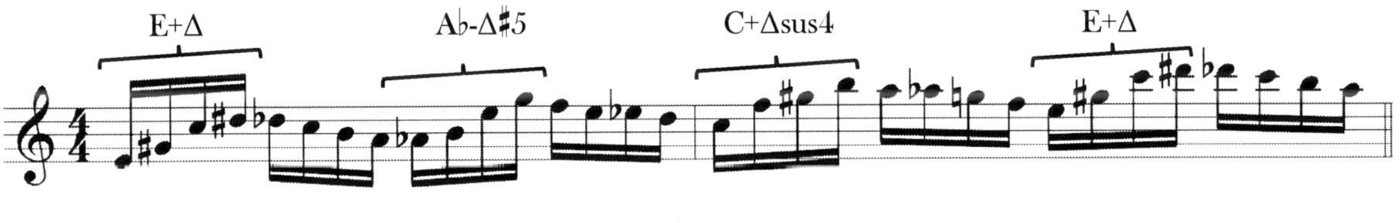

Play in context:

1. Blues
2. Rhythm Changes
3. Another Standard Form

3) Planning Three-Note Ideas

The following ideas create a quite liquid and oblique sound, very much in the style of Tim Miller or Nelson Veras:

Suggested next steps....

1. Develop new patterns with all types of three-note groups
2. Play in all four double-symmetrical augmented scales
3. Change the rhythms of the phrases
4. Create note-grouping patterns
5. Start the same phrases from different rhythmic places
6. Play in context

Example:

Application

Let's take a look at this example using three-note textures on a IΔ VI7alt II-7 V7alt turnaround chord progression:

Next, try using this concept on the following chord changes:

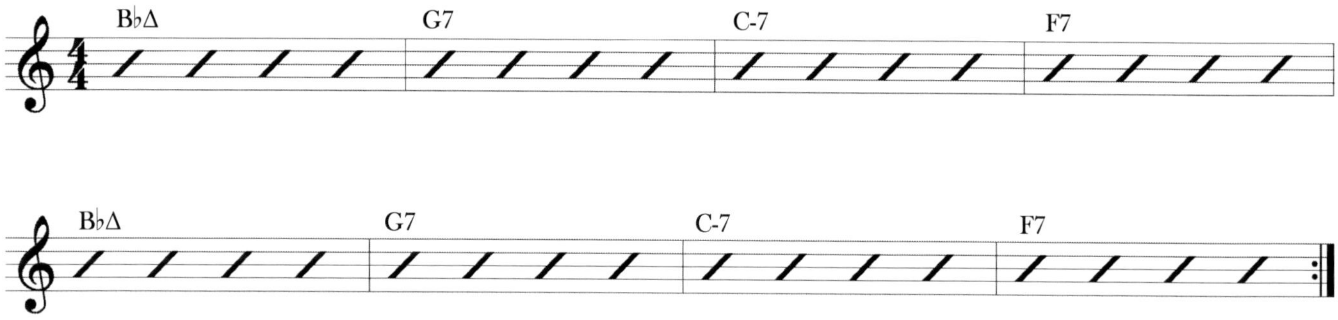

Four-, Five- and Six-Note Texture Examples

Jerry Bergonzi played a pattern with arpeggios ascending and descending diatonically.

Nelson Veras played the following ideas:

1) Maj7 arpeggios ascending in major 3rds.

2) Minor 7 arpeggios ascending and descending in major 3rds.

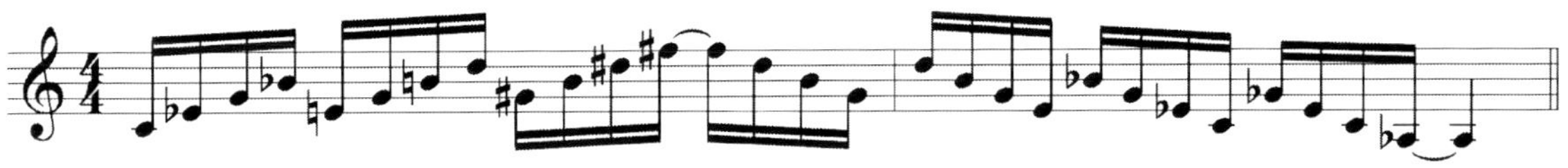

3) 1 2 3 6 texture ascending and descending in major 3rds (Mode 2).

4) C-7 over C major.

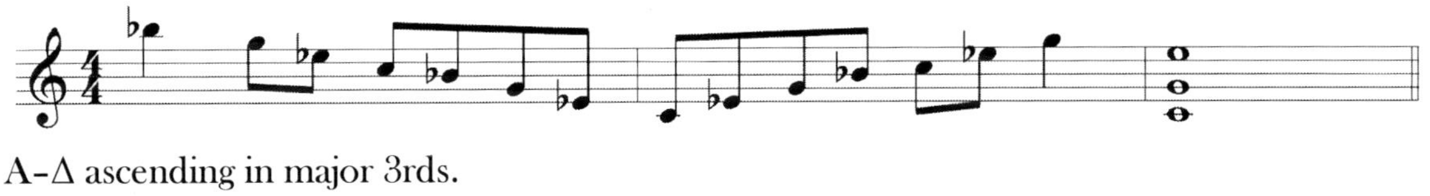

5) A-Δ ascending in major 3rds.

Try this 1 ♭2 3 5 descending pattern featuring the six-note augmented scale followed by a 7 1 3 5 ♭6 ascending pattern in major 3rds:

Isaac Negrene used these two six-note patterns based on the -7 and +Δ arpeggios.

Allan Holdsworth mixed arpeggios with intervals:

1) Intervals + Scale Pattern+ Arpeggios.

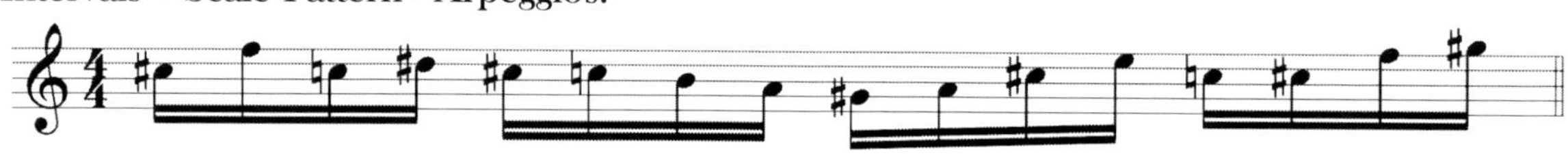

2) Arpeggios + intervals of a third.

3) An arpeggio pattern ascending with a ♯4interval.

4) A pattern featuring second-inversion arpeggios.

Tim Miller and Isaac Romagosa also played different four-note groupings within the same mode:

Mark Turner experimented with a 1 7 ♭7 ♭5 descending pattern.

Here's a permutation of the previous idea: ♯4 1 7 ♭7 (descending).

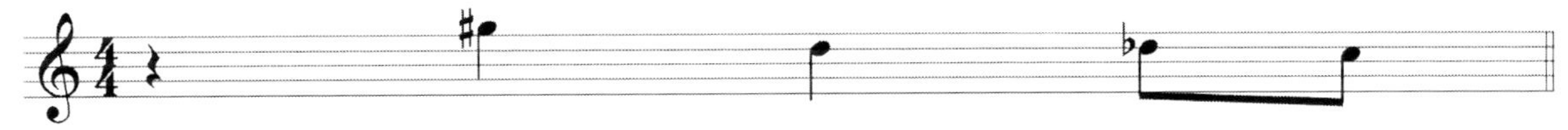

This is a Δ (no 5) add ♯9 pattern in major 3rds with rhythm displacement.

Allan Holdsworth also used a minor arpeggio featuring both a maj7 and a ♭7.

Four-, Five- and Six-Note Texture Exercises

1) Diatonic Arpeggio Patterns:

Suggested next steps....

1. Play diatonic patterns using all of the different arpeggios and triad possibilities
2. Play the same patterns up/up, up/down, down/up, and down/down
3. Play different permutations
4. Play the same patterns in all four double-symmetrical augmented scales
5. Play in context

2) Four-Note Grouping and Pentatonic Exercises:

3) Hexatonic Exercises:

Suggested next steps....

1. Play diatonic patterns using all arpeggio and triad possibilities
2. Play the same patterns up/up, up/down, down/up, and down/down
3. Play different permutations
4. Play the same patterns in all four double-symmetrical augmented scales
5. Play in context

Application

Here's an example of a four-note texture applied to a blues progression:

Try using the same concept on the following chord progression:

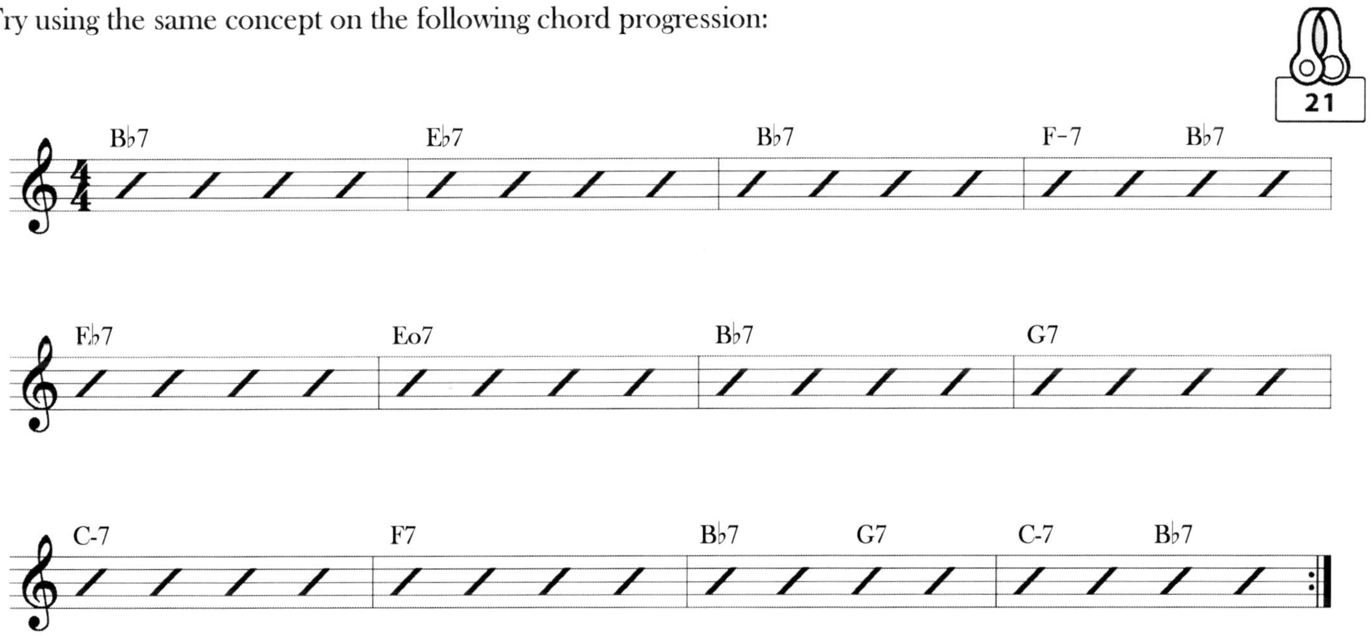

Polychord and Tonal Expansion Examples

Uses of diverse arpeggios from a single mode, spanning an octave or more:

1) FΔ in the first octave and F-Δ♯5 in the second octave.

2) Below are different combinations following the same concept (using Modes 1 and 3):

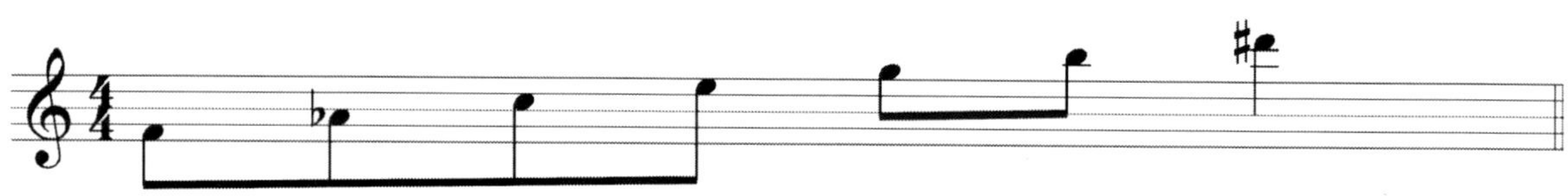

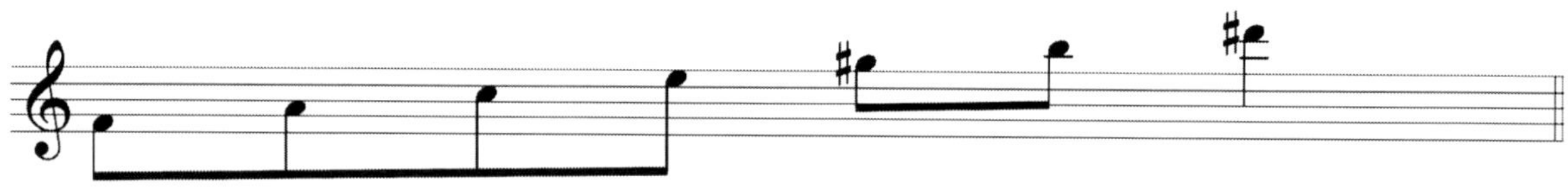

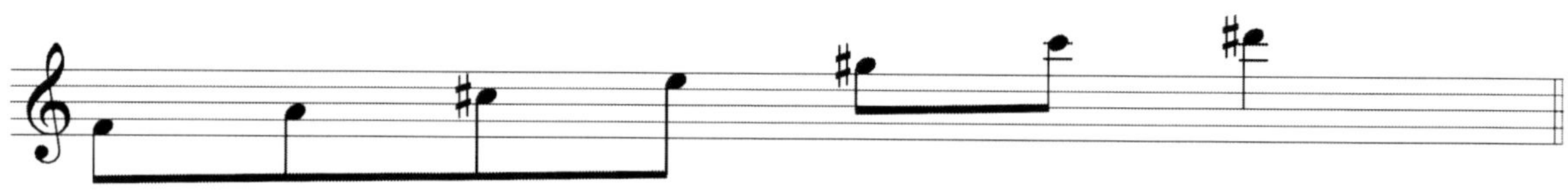

Jerry Bergonzi played various configurations of five-note arpeggios:

1)

2)

Here's an ascending and descending line with tonal expansion:

$\frac{\text{E-}\Delta}{\text{F-}\Delta}$

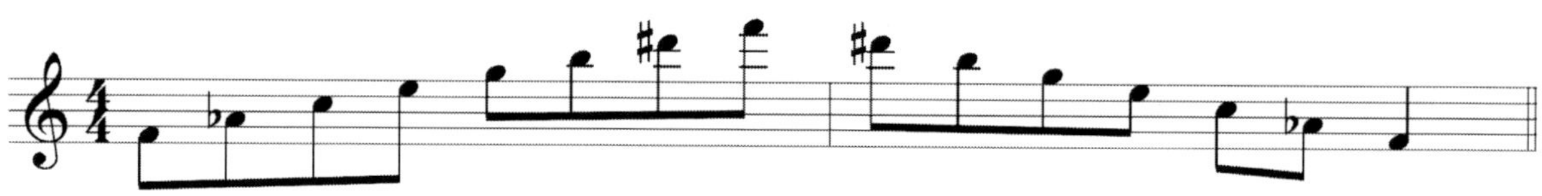

Below are a few examples of sus4, Δ(no5), and sus2 voicings:

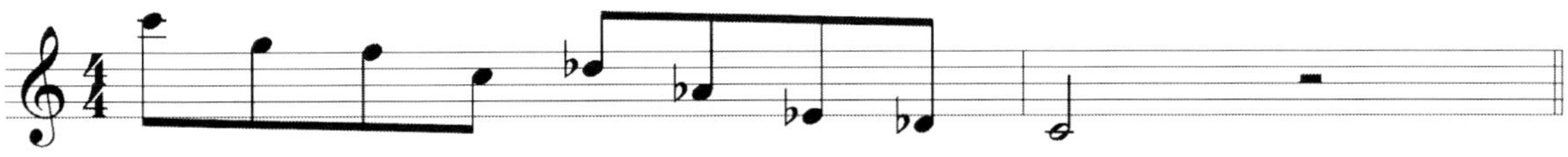

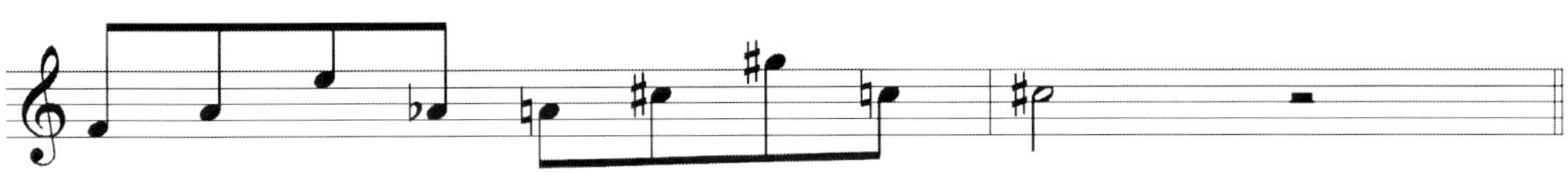

Hubert Nuss used Messiaen polychords as arpeggio lines (tonal expansions):

1) B-Δ / C-7

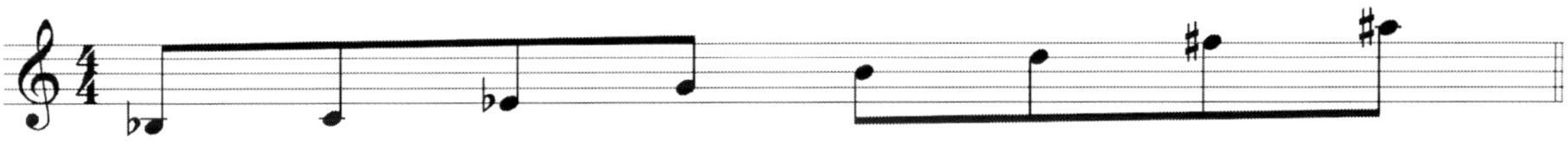

2) C-Δ / E7

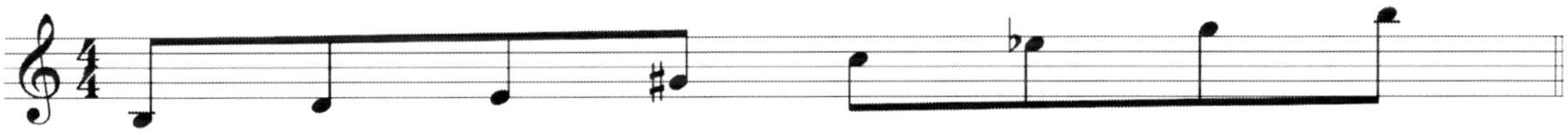

3) E+7 / C-7♭5

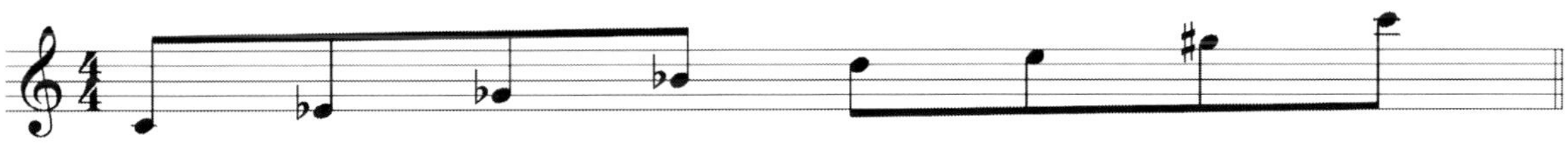

Here's a line by Hubert Nuss which features a B-Δ / C-7 polychord.

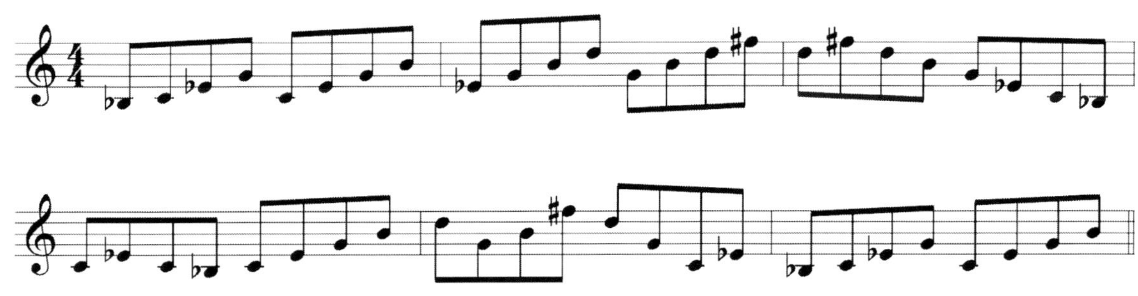

Polychord and Tonal Expansion Exercises

1) Jerry Bergonzi-Inspired Exercises.

Jerry Bergonzi is a legendary sax player and one of the foremost jazz improvisation theorists and educators of our generation.

Suggested next steps....

1. Develop patterns with your own chord selection
2. Play the shapes up/up, up/down, down/up, down/down
3. Play permutations
4. Create diatonic patterns

Pro tip: When using eighth notes, all odd notes from the whole-tone scale and the augmented triad will also belong to the mode we're playing in.

Example:

5. Play rhythm variations
6. Play in context

2) Eight-Note Texture Exercises (Tonal Expansions)

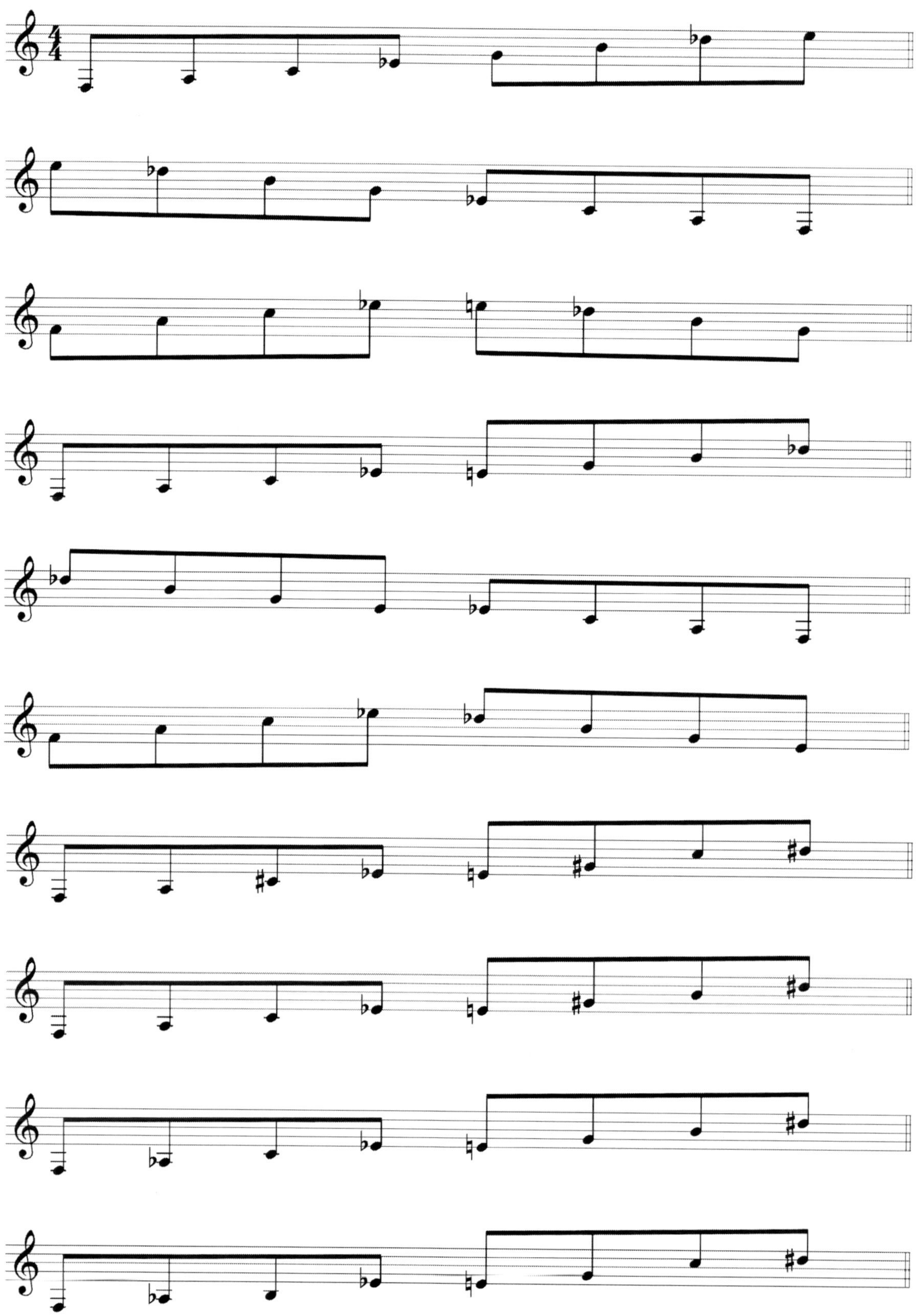

Suggested next steps....

1. Develop patterns from diverse chord selections
2. Play the shapes up/up, up/down, down/up, down/down
3. Play different permutations
4. Create diatonic patterns

Application

Next, let's look at a standard progression with textures made up of polychords and tonal expansions:

InterStella

Try using the same concept on the following chord progression:

23

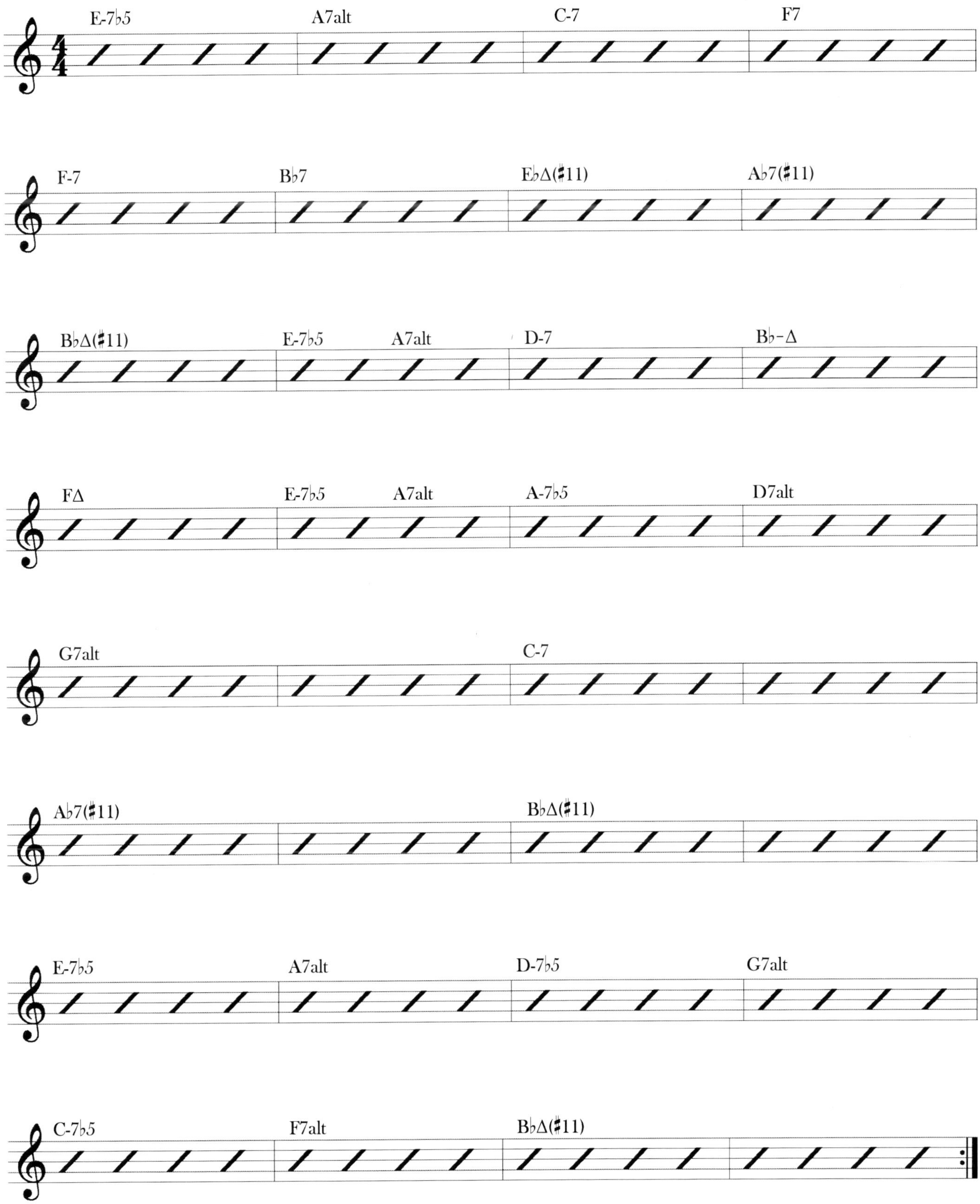

VII. Musical Devices

Tension and Release

In order to successfully improvise with the double-symmetrical augmented scale, you need to know where it's appropriate to play it. When using such a complex musical tool, knowing which part of a given measure or passage you're in is essential to a focused and coherent sound. This is when the concept of *tension and release* comes in handy.

The principle of tension and release tells us that, in a given two-bar structure, the second bar will always build up more tension than the first. Since the double-symmetrical augmented scale is inherently tense, it will often "lie" better in the second bar than on the first. For the release measures I would recommend melodic or arpeggio content.

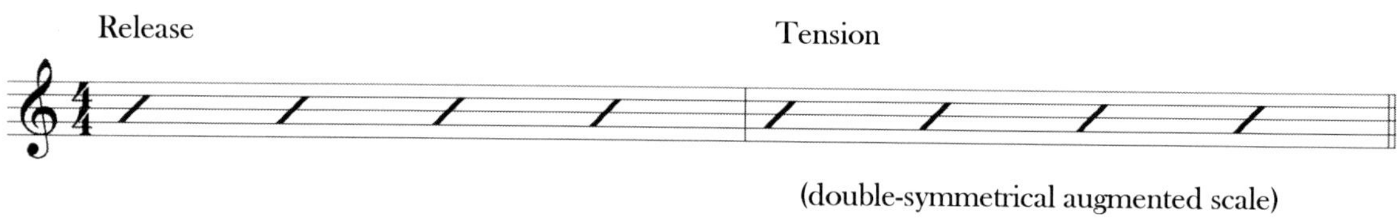

The same concept can be applied to double- or half-bar scenarios.

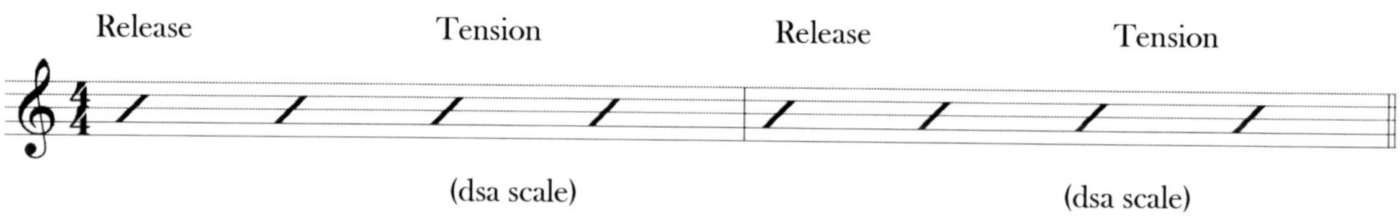

Other options are possible in four-measure scenarios:

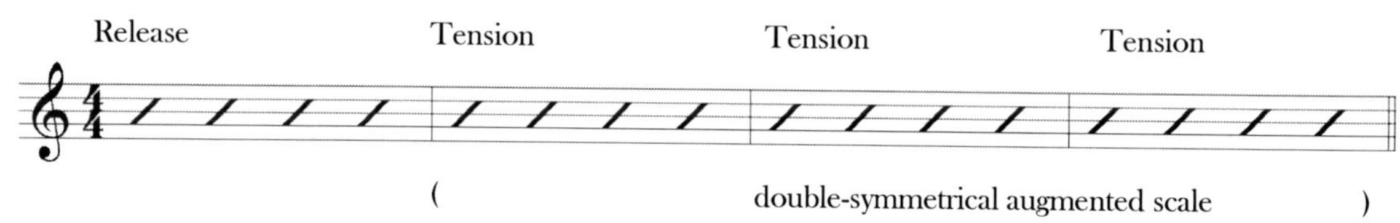

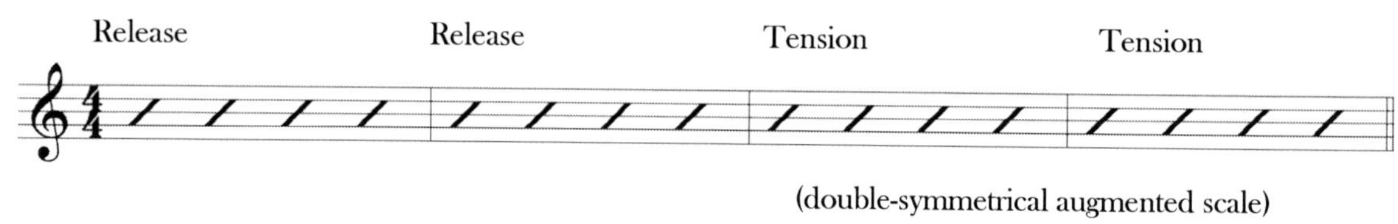

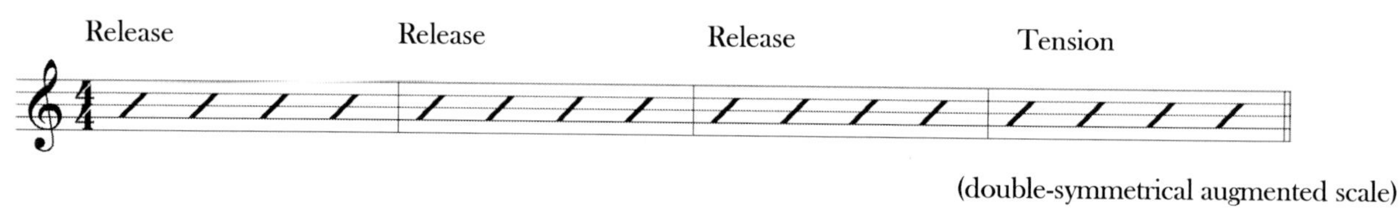

The Double-Symmetrical Augmented Scale in a Modal Context

Let's look at a few possible uses of the double-symmetrical augmented scale in modal or vamp situations. I recommend putting into practice the concept of **access points** and **substitutions**, as explained in chapter IV. You could: 1.) play the double-symmetrical-augmented substitution of the current chord, or 2.) play the double-symmetrical augmented scale of the current chord's implicit dominant.

Example:

Symmetrical What?

The Double-Symmetrical Augmented Scale in a Chord-Scale Relationship

In a chord-scale relationship context, it is essential to keep a balance between diatonic and extratonic sounds ("inside" vs "outside"). You should think about the double-symmetrical augmented scale as one more tool in your toolbox, rather than as a scale that you should be using all the time... That's if you want to keep your brasserie gigs!

That being said, the chord-scale approach is very similar to the modal approach. Applying *tension and release* and *voice leading* principles will make your playing more coherent and consistent. Training your mind to quickly visualize the scale's modes and the substitutions related to each chord will also be an asset.

Here's an example:

Bird Blues Changes

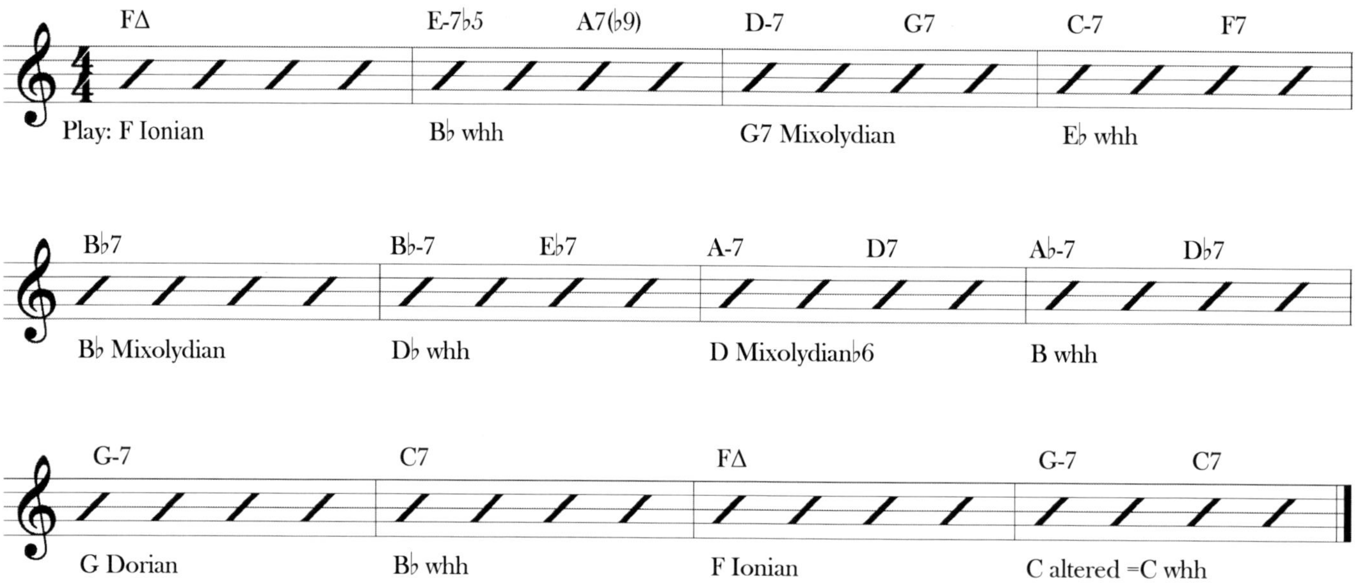

The Double-Symmetrical Augmented Scale in Its Own Diatonic Context

When we encounter a chord progression or musical passage where all chord tones belong to a particular double-symmetrical augmented scale, we can use the same scale throughout.

Here's an example:

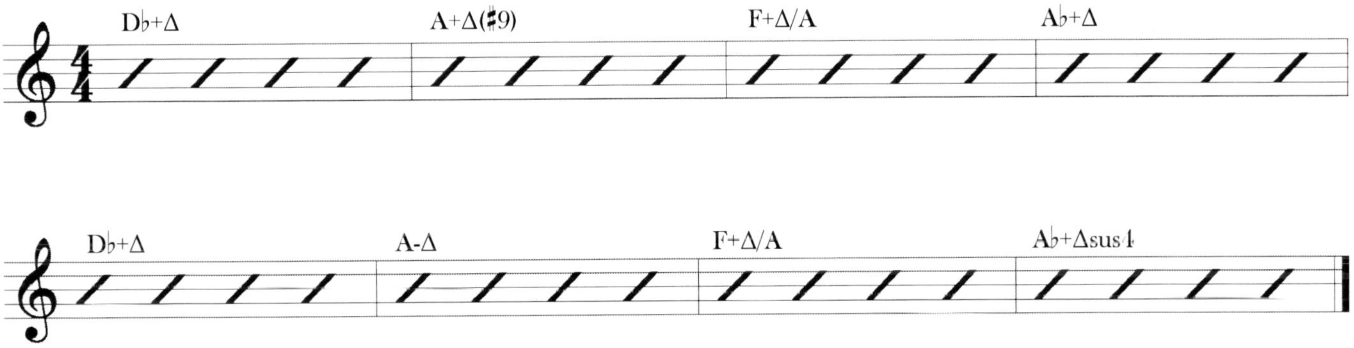

Since all of the chords come from the F=A=D♭ double-symmetrical augmented scale, we can play that same scale throughout the entire progression.

Tonicization (Playing Through Changes)

We also can use the double-symmetrical augmented scale as a long transition (4-8 bars) from one part to another without taking into account the original harmony. This is also known as *playing through changes.*

In this case, you have two options:

1) Using the double-symmetrical augmented scale of the chord until you reach the target chord.

Example:

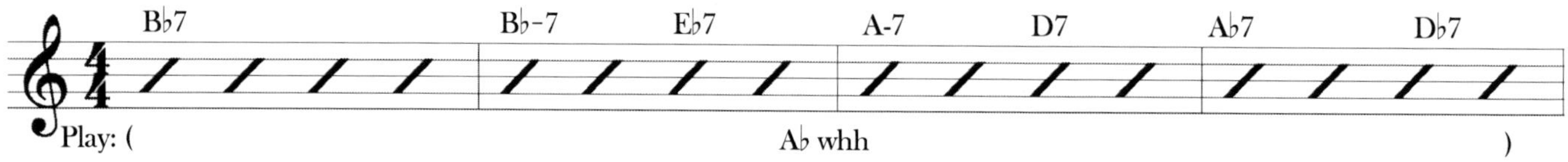

2) Playing the double-symmetrical augmented scale of the target chord.

Example:

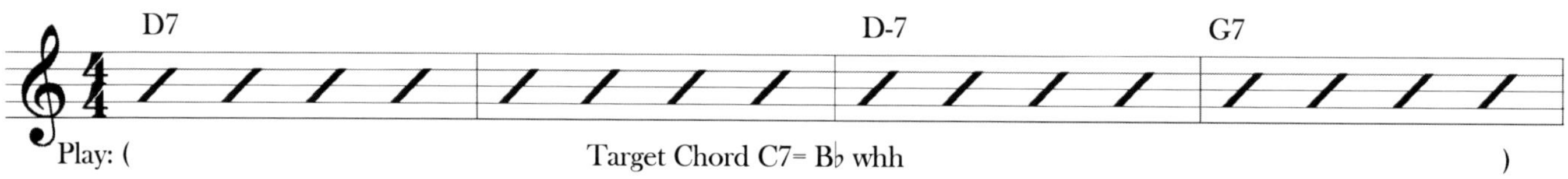

Reharmonizations

As we've already seen, the double-symmetrical augmented scale opens a great deal of possibilities within the impossibilities of typical tonal contexts. For instance, Mode 1 allows for chords which combine up to two different thirds (♭3, 3), three different fifths (♭5, 5, ♯5), and two different sevenths (♭7, 7).

How can we transform these combinations into reharmonization possibilities? As it turns out, this is relatively simple. You just need to find the Lydian, Mixolydian/Lydian ♭7 and Ionian/Phrygian modes relative to the chord you want to reharmonize. These will respectively enable Modes 1, 2 and 3 of the double-symmetrical augmented scale.

Let's examine an example based on Mode 1.

Keep in mind that Mode 1 of the double-symmetrical augmented scale produces the following chord:

Δ (9, ♯9, ♯11,♭13, ♯13)

As the chords repeat themselves every major 3rd, any reharmonization will open up three possibilities. Here's an example in the key of C:

1. CΔ (9,♯9,♯11,♭13,♯13) = CΔ whh
2. EΔ (9,♯9,♯11,♭13,♯13) = EΔ whh
3. A♭Δ (9, ♯9,♯11,♭13,♯13)= A♭Δ whh

If you choose an option which is further from the triad of the original chord, the resulting sound will be more tense. You also have the option to either keep the original bass note or use the bass note of the new chord. Whichever chords you choose, you should always make sure that they work well with the melody.
And now... try it out!

Here's an example of a Mode 1 reharmonization:

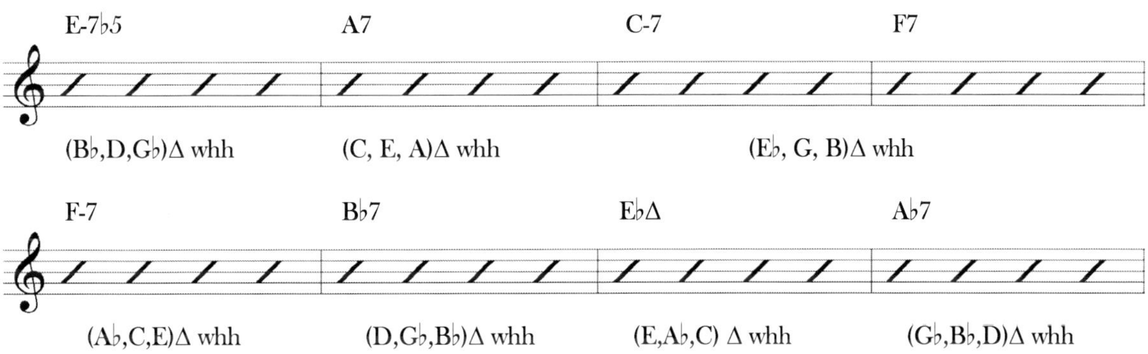

With Voicings:

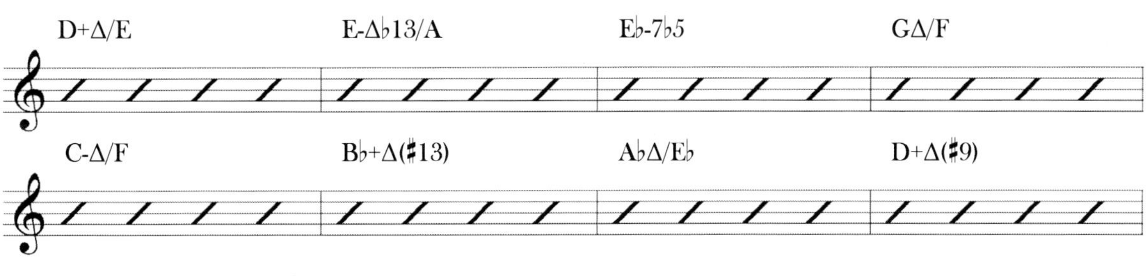

VIII. Uses of the Double-Symmetrical Augmented Scale with Other Symmetrical Scales

Allan Holdsworth and Gary Thomas are two great examples of musicians who combined different symmetrical scales with the double-symmetrical augmented scale.

As an example, the symmetrical diminished scale/whole-half scale (1 2 ♭3 4 ♭5 ♭6 7) fits over mode 1 of the double-symmetrical augmented scale/whole-half-half (1 2 ♭3 3 ♯4 5 ♭6 ♭7 7). This is because both of them contain a -Δ♭5 (diminished maj7 chord). If we arrange the notes that are present in both scales, we get a four-note symmetrical pattern (1 2 ♯4/♭5 ♯5/♭6) that can be used alternatively:

F wh (symmetrical diminished scale)

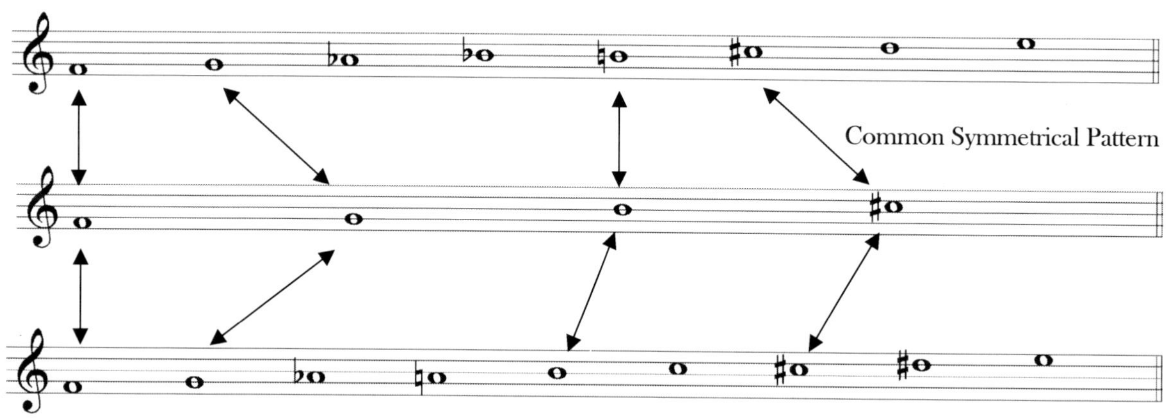

F whh (double-symmetrical augmented scale)

You can also combine cells of F, A or C♯ double-symmetrical augmented scale with F, A or C♯ symmetrical diminished scales.

Let's represent it graphically:

For clarity, we could visualize the double-symmetrical augmented scale as a triangle where the octave is divided in three equal parts:

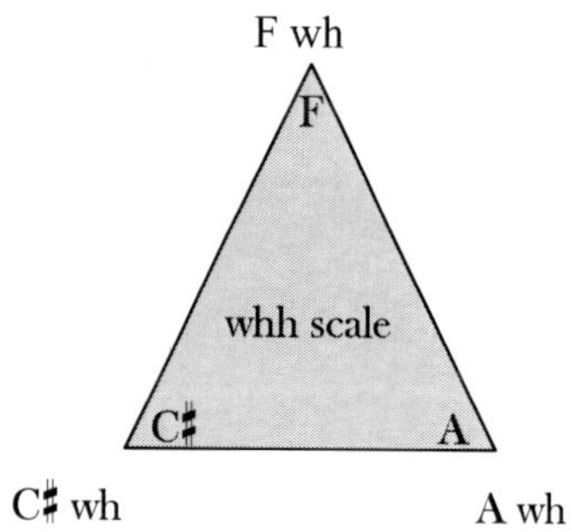

Similarly, we could visualize the symmetrical diminished scale as a square where the octave is divided in four equal parts (minor 3rd symmetry).

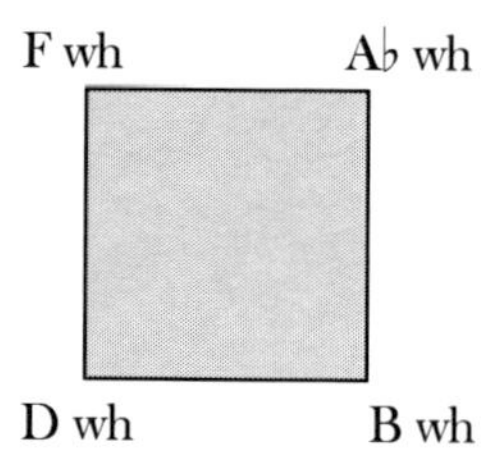

Here are all the possibilities of symmetrical diminished scales from F, A, C♯ double-symmetrical augmented:

F wh = A♭ wh = B wh = D wh (from the F double-symmetrical augmented scale)
A wh = C wh = E♭ wh = G♭ wh (from the A double-symmetrical augmented scale)
C♯ wh = E wh = G wh = B♭ wh (from the C♯ double-symmetrical augmented scale)

The following diagram displays three of the many possibilities within the double-symmetrical augmented and symmetrical diminished scales (same original and target scales).

Example:

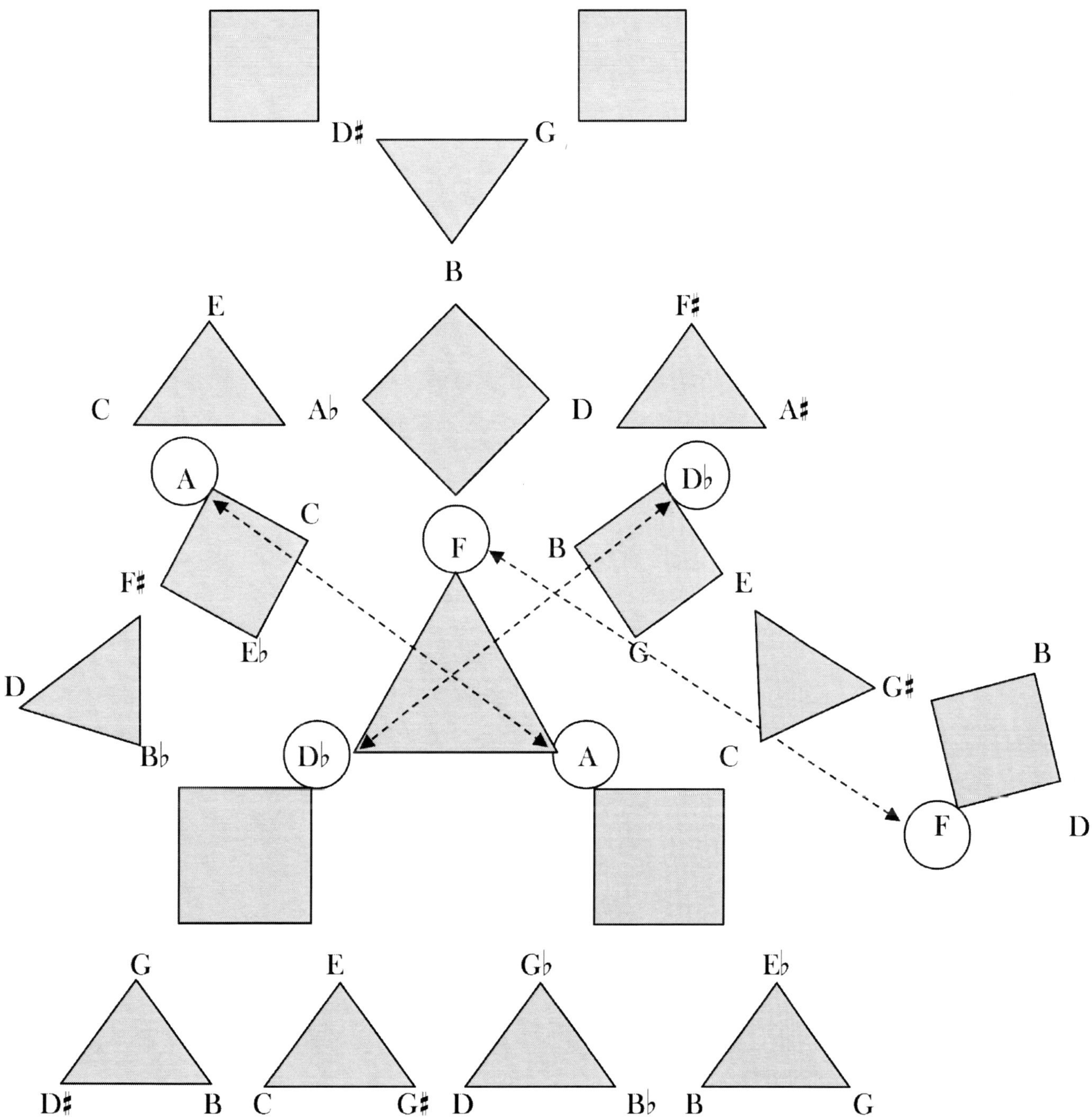

Notes and Observations

Bibliography

Alexander Tcherepnin .... Basic Elements of my Musical Language (http://www.tcherepnin.com)

Allan Holdsworth .... Just for the Curious (Cpp Media Video Transcription Series)

Arnie Berle .... Encyclopedia of Scales, Modes and Melodic Patterns (Mel Bay Publications, Inc.)

Bret Willmott .... Complete Book of Harmony, Theory &Voicing (Mel Bay Publications, Inc.)

Dennis Sandole .... Guitar Lore (Theodore Presser Company)

Gary Keller .... The Jazz Chord Scale Handbook (Advance Music)

Gary Thomas .... A Language Borne of Symmetry Masterclass (www.jazzheaven.com)

Hal Crook .... How to Improvise (Advance Music)

Hubert Nuss .... Messiaen Modes applied to Jazz Harmony (www.jazzheaven.com)

James Collier .... The Making of Jazz: A Comprehensive History (Houghton Mifflin Co.)

Jerry Bergonzi .... Developing a Jazz Language (Advance Music)

Lukas Gabric .... Jazz Course for All Intruments (Mel Bay Publications, Inc.)

L. Dean Bye .... Student's Guide to Music Theory (Mel Bay Publications, Inc.)

L. Dean Bye .... Theory & Harmony for Everyone (Mel Bay Publications, Inc.)

Mike Perlowin .... Music Theory in the Real World (Mel Bay Publications, Inc.)

Nicolas Slominsky .... Thesaurus of Scales and Melodic Patterns (Amsco)

Olivier Messiaen .... Technique de Mon Langage Musical (Alphonse Leduc)

Peter Spitzer .... Jazz Theory Handbook (Mel Bay Publications, Inc.)

Timothy Clarkson .... Chromatic Third Relations in the Improvisations of Mark Turner (Masters of Music Thesis at The Sydney Conservatorium of Music at the University of Sydney)

Conclusion

Congratulations, you made it to the end of my book! Hopefully this is just the beginning of a new world of musical territories for you. The basics explained in this volume are the key to an entire universe, which remains uncharted at the time of this writing. I have no doubt that future research will continue to develop new ideas and applications around the double-symmetrical augmented scale. Meanwhile, I hope that this book will serve as a reference map for your own explorations – and that you enjoy the ride as much as I have.

Xabier Oró